What Others are Saying . . .

"Julie Loar's extended awareness of ancient oracle temples is brought together with a very modern expanded re-interpretation of the subconscious in light of various breakthroughs in science and technology, to deliver a fascinating and quite original approach to dream interpretation— as well as mysterious waking synchronicities—with ideas, stories and imagery that greatly widen the scope of understanding the soul's language as an aid for attaining greater spiritual consciousness. A great read as well as presentation of carefully orchestrated instructions for serious study and reflection on our "para-conscious" mentality—in whatever language we use to describe it."

~ Ted Denmark, PhD, author of award-winning *Winged Messengers*

"In writing *Symbol & Synchronicity: Learning the Soul's Language in Dreams and Waking Life*, Julie Loar has drawn upon her years of in-depth study, metaphysical training, and personal experience to give readers a rich treasure trove of esoteric insights. This heartfelt and highly readable book integrates material from such diverse sources as the Wisdom Traditions of ancient Egypt, the Dream Temples of Greece, and the archetypal work of Carl Jung. Filled with practical, easily applied methods for understanding dreams, symbols, and synchronistic events, Julie has created a helpful, meaningful gift given from her soul to ours."

~ Nancy Chrisbaum, co-author of *Awaken Your Inner Voice: A Guide to Intuition, Dreams, Meditation, Past Lives, and Your Soul's Creative Purpose*

"In following her own inner guidance to write *Symbol & Synchronicity: Learning the Soul's Language in Dreams and Waking Life*, Julie Loar has given readers a highly valuable gift: a practical guide to the life of one's own soul and the messages it delivers to us in a myriad of sometimes mysterious ways. Structured both as a textbook on the inner life of the human body, brain, and psyche and as a handbook to the interpretation of dreams and synchronistic events, Julie's book immediately engages the reader's rational and intuitive faculties. The handbook is distinguished by Julie's new method of dream interpretation, which she calls 'Seven Steps in Dreamwork©.' Complete with a graphically attractive template for creating one's own dream diary and very clear descriptions of the seven steps, this feature of the book will undoubtedly assist many readers to organize and understand their dream lives in beneficial ways. Julie concludes her book by succinctly describing, using her seven-step process, a series of dreams and synchronicities that profoundly changed her life, and led her to writing this book. Full of fascinating anecdotes and well-chosen quotes from the works of other influential authors, *Symbol & Synchronicity: Learning the Soul's Language in Dreams and Waking Life*, will surely help any sincere reader to learn the language of her or his soul."

~ Ed Conroy, author of *Report on Communion*

"Julie Loar's *Symbol & Synchronicity: Learning the Soul's Language in Dreams and Waking Life* is extraordinary—her knowledge is vast, and the timing is Spirit Divine. Tracking my dreams with her *Seven Steps in Dreamwork©* process has been revealing and meaningful, some were actual epiphanies. It has inspired me in many wonderful ways to expand and be truer and truer to my Beloved Soul's joyful fulfillment of that for which I came. It's need to serve, and call to be loyal – is tugging more and more. The descriptions of her own experiences, and processes that happened while writing the book, feels like I could have written your same words about book process. The teaching is exceptional, and arouses curiosity in one to go deeper with science and mystical interests. There is merit here for everyone, no matter where they are on their path. The sharing of experiences is very valuable and makes it so real. The book is a gem." '

~ Candace Newman, author of *Your Inner River of Peace: Ten Messages of Love*

"Julie Loar understands the universe within which we exist. In *Symbol & Synchronicity: Learning the Soul's Language in Dreams and Waking Life*, she provides a mechanism of enhancing a conscious recognition of the world by using our personal environment as an Oracle.

"She supports her program and process through study and review of ancient artifacts and history. Brilliance commences manifestation where she integrates and mingles profound inspiration gained through otherworldly knowledge, which expands into divine advice and prophecy.

"Her personal experiences culminate into cognizant, and ethereal messages, which support her uncanny ability to create an opening of conscious awareness in the clouds of suppression and cynical messages that stream in from unhealthy voices inundating our worldview. Using both rationality and logic with intuitive processing, she uses a mindful approach through dreams, visions, and synchronicities that transfer vital information via the universe that is constantly speaking to us.

\

"You could use Julie's extraordinary work as a college course to satisfy your intellectual curiosity. But, if the acceleration of your Spiritual Path is important, then move ever deeper into a discovery of your Soul's innate power. Become amazed with your command, and mastery of discernment by using Julie's *Seven Steps in Dreamwork*© plan of action to shut out superfluous noise. If you choose to grow in conscious awareness, the wisdom flowing through this book will spark your journey, in an exponential manner. I cannot recommend any work of written art with any greater value—A+."

~ Constance d'Angelis, JD, author of *The 7 Laws of Inner Peace*

"*Symbol & Synchronicity: Learning the Soul's Language in Dreams and Waking Life* is *the* book I would want to have if shipwrecked on a desert island. It opens the door to dreams in a way no other book has done for me. Using the foundation of history, myth, science, and examples of ancient dreams and dreamers, Julie's thoughtful method of Record, Reflect, and Resolve in her *Seven Steps in Dreamwork*©, creates a very accessible platform to remember and analyze my own dreams. With her conscientious guidance, I have been able to use the power of symbolism with even more depth as I navigate my own dream life, and bring those messages into my daily life. It doesn't matter if the reader is a "beginner" or "master," this book has the pathway to appreciate, interpret, and embrace the power of dreams."

~ Susan Andra Lion, author of *Night Threads, a Weaving of Soul Stories from the Dreamtime* and *Fox Light, Magic Hidden in Plain Sight*

Symbol & Synchronicity

Learning the Soul's Language
in Dreams and Waking Life

Julie Loar

Satiama
PUBLISHING

Out of Darkness into Dawn

For Ariel, Lioness of God,

Voice of my Soul

Spiral

Karen Stuth

I met myself while walking
up a gradually narrowing spiral
unfolding like the unbroken peel
of an apple's skin
drawn upward
a well-worn walking stick in hand
as I realized
so gradually I almost missed it
that I was traveling in circles
through space and time

At times the footpath was wide and receiving
beautiful, bejeweled, inviting
other places offering a familiar difficulty
slippery and choked with branches and thorns
that left me bleeding
with gaps I had to jump over
often narrow and terrifying
so that I closed my eyes in terror
my fear of heights taking on a new meaning
as I finally comprehended the true nature of my phobia

I reached out my hand
hoping to touch my own arm
in comfort and support
as I passed myself again and again
but now more than a few rounds ahead
I knew I was leaving behind
the concept of me
a two-dimensional character in a worn-out tale
my old stories cast aside
a past of regret disappearing behind me
like earthy, pungent wood smoke
as I moved up

My legs often trembled
as I walked and climbed
around and around
and around
each completed circle surprising me
with something I had already encountered

but perhaps not fully resolved
I moved through and past those painful places
greeting them as timeworn friends
so ancient and old

Invisible hands reached out to support me
when my willingness flagged
I was astonished to realize
unseen companions accompanying me on this climb
for time outside of memory and imagination
as I realized I had never been travelling alone

Moving now in ever smaller circles
I watched myself gain more vertical purchase
the space between my selves
sometimes appearing close
other times as if we were on different planes
a living Escher painting

Stopping to catch my breath
I found myself wanting to look back
to see how far I had come
but at one look down
would show me a past already disappeared into ether
and my ancient self no longer there either
gone away into the dreamscape
that was never actually real

It wasn't oxygen I was lacking
as the air grew richer and warmer
but the absence of pain and angst
as I moved up my soul's spiral staircase
the climbing now easier
an unseen sun warming my face
obstacles barely registering
as I passed them by without acknowledgement

The top of the spiral was no longer a destination
but an eternal aspiration
as I continued to climb
toward my immoveable
never-ending destiny

Contents

Foreword

When as a high school student having lunch in the cafeteria, Henry, an African-American friend of mine, approached me with a book in his hand. This was a copy of Max Heidel's incredible work, *The Rosicrucian Cosmo Conception*. "You know Alan," he began, "from some of our conversations, I think you should read this book."

That was 1958, and we were both 14 years old. I borrowed Henry's book and soon realized I was not ready to read it (I finally did—and it made sense—some 15 years or so later). But there was one word in the "Cosmo Conception" that did stand out to me as a mystically curious boy—and still does to this day as a mystically dedicated man— and that word is "consciousness."

In her latest book, *Symbol & Synchronicity: Learning the Soul's Language in Dreams and Waking Life*, Julie Loar has beautifully explored the various levels of human consciousness, giving structure (Julie is a Capricorn, after all!), and a precise link between intuitive perception and the personal experience of consciousness through a clear intellectual presentation of same. This link between "intuition and intellect" is at the heart of the union of the Soul and the personality along our common Path to Initiation.

Among the many seers, philosophers, and astrologers who have affected my life and work, two stand out with great prominence. The first is the Master Djwal Khul, who in his amazing book, *Esoteric Astrology*, reminds us that astrology is "the science of *effective energies*" (italics mine). The second of these great Teachers is Dr. Carl Jung, the master psychologist, mystic, and interpreter of dreams, who brought the concept of the range and interconnection of human archetypes (certainly seeded by the Ancient Greeks) to the doors of modern astrological and psychological thinking.

Julie Loar is a dedicated student of both of these master teachers, and this book is a reflection of these decades of study in terms of the Ancient Wisdom Teachings and the importance of dream work along the road to self-awareness. Bravo, Julie Loar—thank you for this wonderful contribution to the One Work that we share.

Alan Oken
Bali, Indonesia
April 21, 2021

Introduction

When the student is ready the teacher will appear.

When the student is truly ready the teacher will disappear.

~ Lao Tzu, *Tao Te Ching*

I woke on a snowy morning in mid-March of 2020 as the world imploded in the midst of a global pandemic. On this March morning near spring equinox worst case scenarios were being examined, and the situation was grim that the US would have what was needed to address the crisis. Millions lost jobs, businesses and schools locked down, and news was more foreboding each day.

And on that snowy morning I woke from a vivid dream that felt like a "call." I titled the dream *Messenger Bag*. In the dream, which is described and interpreted in Chapter 13, I carried every bit of my work, worth, and identity in a saddle-colored messenger bag. Historically, these bags have been used by Roman legionnaires, army medics, electronics repair people, and college students. Messenger bags are still in widespread use by letter carriers, who rode horses in earlier times, then bicycles, and now trucks, faithfully carrying and delivering their messages.

The messenger bag in my dream contained my wallet and passport and was stuffed with papers and projects—every bit of my life's work past, present, and future. My first book was titled *Messengers*, so the symbol had layers of meaning. In the dream I kept putting the heavy bag down, and forgetting to take it with me, as I searched for a way to get fed. The meal I had was unappetizing and not nutritious: I wanted and needed more—in the dream I set off to find something that would satisfy my needs.

The simple interpretation of the dream is I have a great deal of work that needs attention and shouldn't be ignored or forgotten. I should pay attention to the work as this is what will "feed me." This book is part of the answer to what felt like a clarion call of guidance.

Symbol & Synchronicity: Learning the Soul's Language in Dreams and Waking Life was meant to follow the *Sky Lore Anthology*, which was compiled and self-published during the first six weeks of the pandemic lockdown as the first response to the not-so-subtle message in the dream. The present book was originally meant to contain a similar collection of earlier articles on dreams. After the Vellum software learning curve, and the daunting task of the *Sky Lore Anthology* books, arranging three dozen or so of my former dream articles seemed simple by contrast. But the Muse, my Soul, had other ideas, and the journey of this book has taken me to unexpected places with surprising gifts, huge blessings, as well as daunting challenges.

Symbol & Synchronicity is divided into five parts. The first section recounts teachings of ancient wisdom, describes famous oracle sites, leading edge research in quantum physics, and how that impacts human consciousness. I share a diagram of the Anatomy of the Psyche that came in meditation and offer new terms to describe the aspects of consciousness. Section two explores the fundamentals of dream work, including symbolism, types of dreams and other nighttime experiences, as well as the amazing phenomena of synchronicity and serendipity. Section three dives deep into the real work of dream interpretation and offers a *Seven Steps in Dreamwork*© process to work with dreams that was revealed as a result of a powerful dream. Section four contains five chapters with resource lists and descriptions of traditional meanings of many symbols. Section five offers practical tools for enriching your own dream work, including instructions for creating your own dream oracle temple.

Everyone dreams, but few of us know how to decode the symbolic messages that come while we sleep or appear in waking moments of synchronicity or serendipity. Every culture and tradition in the world pays attention to dreams. A universal understanding seems to exist that guidance offered through dreams comes from a wiser place, a deeper knowing, than our everyday awareness alone can provide. Perhaps this is because our logical "rational" mind is disengaged while we sleep, and our subconscious only reflects honest feedback that comes from the level of our Higher Self.

The journey of life is not a random dance of atoms within the flow of space-time, but is instead a grand plan called evolution. We move through eons, gathering experience, learning our lessons, and slowly growing into our potential. Dreams, synchronicities, and the magic of serendipity have always provided guidance, but it was only priestesses and healers at famous oracle sites, or shamans, who could decode the symbols. In more recent times, such gifted teachers as C. G. Jung and Marie-Louise von-Franz offered amazing wisdom that now guides the work of many therapists and has certainly inspired me. However, as we walk the spiritual Path, I believe we can learn to be our own oracles, forming a conscious connection with our Soul, and learning to understand and interpret the symbolic language ourselves.

What if you knew you had your own personal and trusted guide, standing ready to shed light on your path and bring messages of encouragement? Your guide would show you how to live a better life and reveal your greatest stumbling blocks, holding up a mirror to reflect the consequences of your choices. Wouldn't you listen? Dreams and synchronicities can act in just this way, becoming powerful guides if we learn to understand the language of these symbolic messengers, which I believe are the wise voice of our Soul.

It has been a passion to understand how the language of symbols, and the messages that we receive through dreams and synchronicities, can transform our lives. I've interpreted dreams live on national radio and authored an award-winning book describing how to use Tarot to interpret dreams. Even though I have worked with dreams for decades, as I walked the daily path of writing this book I realized that I was being worked upon by the process as much as I worked on the book.

Several fundamental assumptions are key to this work and certainly to my approach to life and learning. These ideas are informed by years of study, drawing on the deep reservoir of Earth's cultures, ancient wisdom, and teachers I admire. What has emerged from writing this book is a broader exploration of the subject of guidance, the spiritual path, and how we might become more attuned to what I have come to call the "Voice of the Soul." Several fundamental assumptions are key to this work and certainly to my approach to life and learning. These ideas are informed by years of study, drawing on the deep reservoir of Earth's cultures, ancient wisdom, and teachers I admire. What has emerged from writing this book is a broader exploration of the subject of guidance, the spiritual path, and how we might become more attuned to what I have come to call the "Voice of the Soul."

My essential premise is that our waking consciousness can learn to form a powerful dialog with our Soul, our wise and eternal guide, through the agency of our subconscious. The connecting link is already there, but we must learn to recognize the voice and listen. Once the link is conscious, and the symbolic language learned, the feedback mechanism is profound. When our Psyche is operating as intended this profoundly informs our growth and sheds light on our spiritual path, accelerating our progress. We are not alone on this journey through time. Our Soul is always with us and within us, acting as wise guide and guardian. The purpose of this book is to strengthen that connection.

Paying attention to our dreams has the potential to help us in ordinary life as well as guiding our spiritual journey. Teachings have been described by many wisdom traditions and left as a legacy by those who have traveled this way before, gifting us with an explanation of the Way. We are meant to awaken and grow into our spiritual potential This book hopes to share the journey, the map, the guide, and wisdom for ancient traditions and modern teachers—footprints on the Path left by those who have walked this way before.

The counsel offered through our dreams and waking synchronicities is free and provides a priceless opportunity to commune with the wisest part of our being. When we actively work with our dreams our ability to decode the symbolic language becomes fluent, and taking the extra step to learn personal dream symbols profoundly deepens the wise counsel. If we spend time to learn the symbolic language, and expect this wise counsel, we will be amply rewarded. All that is asked is time and an earnest heart to open a dialog with our Higher Self, the voice of our Soul, the aspect of our being that lives in eternity.

My journey has been framed by the miracle of amazing dreams, powerful signs, and the magic of synchronicity and serendipity. I have experienced the power of the practice—not just theory—that I write about in a way that is not academic, and I believe these messages have been the clear voice of my Soul. At critical points along the way I received guidance in just the way I hope you, the reader, will on your own path. I have listened to the counsel, and done my best to act on the wise advice. As a result, I have been transformed; I am not the same person who began this book a year ago.

If you have embarked upon a conscious spiritual path, it is my hope that you will find insight along the way in the pages of this book. If we can become our own oracle, learning the language of our Soul, and hearing the voice, the way becomes clearer. I invite you to come along on a journey of discovery, becoming fluent in the symbolic language of your Soul, and opening a conscious dialog with your Soul, your eternal self.

Note: This book is not meant to replace traditional therapy or the advice of a physician in the case of a serious physical or emotional problem.

Part One

Ancient Wisdom & Modern Knowledge

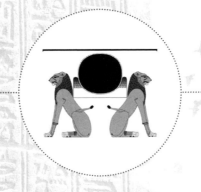

He that is beneath

I have seen the Moon fill with rain like a silver cup,
and I have sailed my boat over heaven.
I am the Sun, roaring between two lions named
Yesterday and Tomorrow.

~ Normandi Ellis, *Awakening Osiris: The Egyptian Book of the Dead*

CHAPTER ONE

Symbol & Synchronicity: A Golden Scarab

*Synchronicity reveals the meaningful connection
between the subjective and objective world.*

~ C. G. Jung, *Synchronicity*

The inspiration for the wider lens of this book comes from a story in *Synchronicity*, by Swiss psychoanalyst Dr. Carl G. Jung. It's a favorite story of mine about a golden scarab, which is a stunning example of how dream symbols and synchronicities conspire to wake us from a state of unconsciousness. The event in the story was also key to the genesis of the now-famous concept of synchronicity. Dr. Jung tells the story of a young woman patient who was at a critical juncture in her treatment.

> My example concerns a young woman patient who, in spite of efforts made on both sides, proved to be psychologically inaccessible. The difficulty lay in the fact that she always knew better about everything. Her excellent education had provided her with a weapon ideally suited to this purpose, namely a highly polished Cartesian rationalism with an impeccably "geometrical" idea of reality. After several fruitless attempts to sweeten her rationalism with a somewhat more human understanding, I had to hope that something unexpected and irrational would turn up, something that would burst the intellectual retort into which she had sealed herself.
>
> Well, I was sitting opposite her one day, with my back to the window, listening to her flow of rhetoric. She had an impressive dream the night before where someone had given her a golden

scarab — a costly piece of jewelry. While she was telling me this dream, I heard something behind me gently tapping on the window. I turned around and saw a fairly large flying insect knocking against the window-pane from outside in the obvious effort to get into the dark room. This seemed very strange. I opened the window immediately and caught the insect in the air as it flew in. It was a *scarabaeid* beetle, a common rose-chafer (*Cetonia aurata*), whose gold-green color nearly resembles that of a golden scarab. I handed the beetle to my patient with the words, "Here is your scarab." This experience punctured the desired hole in her rationalism and broke the ice of her intellectual resistance. The treatment could now be continued with satisfactory results.

Dr. Jung called the incident a "discovery produced by the coincidental and synchronous appearance and occurrence of the golden scarab in the patient's dream coupled with the highly unlikely appearance of a scarab during her session." Jung coined the term synchronicity to describe the "temporally coincident occurrences of acausal events." The term means "together in time" from the Greek *syn* "together" and *chronus* "time."

Jung felt the principle of synchronicity encompassed his concept of the collective unconscious because it described a governing dynamic that underlay all of human experience. He said that "synchronicity indicates that coincidences are more than chance, less than causality, a confluence of events in a numinous or awesome atmosphere."

He became convinced that synchronicities arose during points of crisis in people's lives and contained insights for future growth and development. Jung said "If ESP is real we must conclude that besides the connection between cause and effect there is another factor in nature that expresses itself in the arrangement of events and appears as meaning."

In the example, the young woman's dream was the medium, or transmitter of the message, the golden scarab was the symbol, and the beetle at Jung's window was the synchronicity. The dream scarab and the flying beetle came "together in time" to deliver a shock to the young woman's waking consciousness and was a message too powerful to ignore. With a live beetle in her hand the young woman chose to accept the symbolic gift, the synchronicity offered, and the real work of analysis and growth could begin.

The ancient Egyptians saw the scarab *(Scarabaeus sacer)* as a symbol of renewal, rebirth, and transformation. The beetle was symbolically associated with the rising sun god Ra Khefer because scarab beetles roll large balls of dung in which the females lay their eggs. At sunrise, as the dung warms, the newborn beetles fly out of their humble origins. Like the lotus with its roots in mud, opening its petals to the Sun, newborn dung beetles rise from the raw earthly substance of the world in an act of spontaneous self-creation. They spread their wings and rise into the light, giving birth to new creatures.

The Egyptians saw a parallel in the birth of the dung beetle to the progression of the Sun through the sky from east to west each day. As the newborn sun god rose each morning, he brought light and life to the land. The connection between the beetle and the sun was so close symbolically that the young sun god was thought to be reborn in the form of a winged scarab beetle every morning at sunrise. To the ancient Egyptians, the cycle of the sun through the day, night, and year represented the journey of the soul through earthly life and eternity. Life on Earth was full of lessons meant to prepare us for eternity.

The rising Sun represented victory over darkness. What is usually called the *Book of the Dead*, because papyrus scrolls were found with Egyptian burials, was actually named the *Book of Coming Forth into the Light of Amun Ra*. At dawn the Sun was Ra Khefer, new born light. At noon the Sun was Ra Horacthi, victorious over darkness. At sunset the Sun was called Ra Atum and was seen as an old man. During the night, when the Sun journeyed into the underworld, this was considered a metaphor for the darkness of earthly life.

Once interpreted, the golden scarab symbol might have powerfully suggested to Jung's young patient that instead of the rarified intellectual atmosphere where she was "stuck" she might look into the seemingly more mundane and earthy aspects of life. The expensive golden scarab jewelry gifted to her in the dream could be seen as an offering to do the work with a rich reward, and a symbol of coming out of darkness into light and insight, awakening to the change of mind that needed to occur. When we are receptive, our own versions of golden scarabs will appear in our lives, and it is the vision of this book that they will.

A synchronicity occurs when two events happen simultaneously that appear to be causally unrelated. And, the chance that they would occur together at random, or by chance, should be very small. As noted above, the word stems from two Greek words, *syn* "together" and *chronos* "time," together in time. One interpretation is that events are merely coincidence, chance occurrences, but with a real synchronicity the emotional reaction is so strong and the import is overwhelming. Rather than chance there is a powerful feeling of meaning and connectedness. Albert Einstein had a term in quantum physics called entanglement, which he described as "spooky action at a distance." He was so puzzled by the concept he thought it must be impossible. There is much we still do not understand about the Universe, our own consciousness, and how we are connected to all that is. Remaining open to new revelations is always wise.

Learning to watch for signs and symbols, especially powerful synchronicities, can offer guidance on our path of awakening. Synchronicities are like waking dreams, powerful symbolic messages that occur in the waking state. Our Soul informs our conscious awareness through the agency of dream symbols and synchronicities and breaks though to our conscious awareness, sometimes with a shock. Once we engage with this powerful experience, we invite more such occurrences and our guidance increases.

Symbol

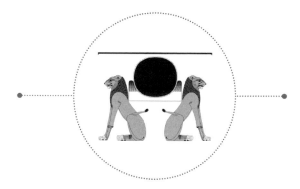

Aker – Yesterday (Duaj) & Tomorrow (Sefer)
"He who is beneath"

I had a powerful synchronicity experience on August 15-16, 2020 while working on this book. This exact date in the year 2020 marks the helical rising of Sirius, when the brightest star in the sky rises before the Sun, sparkling in lingering darkness before dawn. I'm sorry to say I did not rise to watch. Thousands of years ago due to precession, the slow backward apparent motion of the stars, this event happened at summer solstice; now this happens in mid-August.

In ancient Egypt this event marked the beginning of the sacred year when the star of Isis, queen of magic and master of words of power, rose before the Sun. In ancient times this heralded the new year and the onset of the annual Nile flood. This was a truly important time as Sirius, Sothis to the Egyptians, and the most important star in sky, became visible after seventy days in the underworld. Sirius rising in east meant the goddess had returned.

On this August day, as part of my ongoing research, I listened to an audio lecture about Dreams and Death by scholar and Jungian analyst Dr. Marie-Louise von Franz. In her lecture, where she read a paper from content of her book of the same name, she spoke of the ancient Egyptian twin lion deity Aker, pictured above.

Ancient Egyptians lived in a world of magic and saw symbols and significance everywhere. As a lifetime student of Egyptian mysteries, I have long been intrigued with the Aker symbol. Aker is an extremely old Egyptian god depicted as two lions with the solar orb in between, resting on the horizon. His name means "he who is beneath," and the names of the two lions are Duaj, "yesterday" and Sefer, "tomorrow." The solar orb in the center represents the present moment. One lion faces west, where the Sun enters the underworld at sunset, and the other faces east where the Sun emerges out of darkness at dawn.

To the Egyptians, the daily journey of the Sun represented the journey of the soul through time. In addition to guarding the gates of sunrise and sunset the Aker lions watched over the boat of the sun god Ra as he made his nightly and perilous journey through the underworld—the world of dreams and death. *Duaj* protected the sun god as he entered the gate of sunset each evening, and *Sefer* assured that the dawn birth of the newborn sun god, Ra Khefer, portrayed as a winged scarab, took place each morning. This brought the new day into being as well as symbolically bringing the soul out of darkness into light.

Von Franz authored twenty books that included the subjects of Egypt, alchemy, and archetypes, among others, and interpreted 65,000 dreams in her clinical work with clients. She translated many alchemical texts for C. G. Jung during the long years of their collaboration. She believed the symbolic significance of Aker was "the invisible part of the conscious and the visible part of the subconscious." To say that I was intrigued would be an understatement. Since the meaning of Aker's name is "he that is beneath" this symbolically represents the underworld of our Psyche and therefore is the realm of the subconscious. Here is rich meaning as the nightly journey of the Sun, and the soul through the world of dreams, is a territory and genesis of profound symbolic significance.

Von Franz also mentioned, which I had not recalled, that the stages of alchemical transformation exactly matched the stages of mummification of Osiris, which lasted 70 days. These stages are listed in what are known as the *Coffin Texts*. The number 70 is significant as that is the period of invisibility of Sirius mentioned above. Osiris was the god of the dead and the underworld, although the mysteries of his cult had more to do with rebirth and the annual resurrection of the land of Egypt. It's worth noting that the ancient name of Egypt was *Khem*, and is the origin of the word alchemy, and will be discussed in a later chapter. I was amazed that I was prompted to study this material on this auspicious day.

Synchronicity

This same morning, August 16, 2020, as I was deep into researching the twin lion Aker symbol for the *Symbol & Synchronicity: Learning the Soul's Language in Dreams and Waking Life* book in progress, I received a text message from my daughter Elizabeth. The text included a picture of her with two young cats that were recently adopted by her friend John. Seeing her between two felines, was a startling synchronicity. I cannot comprehend the incalculable odds that the text message of two cats with a central figure should arrive at the same moment I was studying the Aker symbol. And further, that I was deep into Egyptian mysticism the same day that Sirius rose before the Sun. That would have been a momentous day for me in one of my ancient Egyptian lives, and the symbolic messages are stunning.

Later that evening when I discussed the day's intriguing and synchronous events with my husband Ted, who was in California at the time, he said he had just heard two bobcats near the road. That had never happened before, and he was amazed when he heard them "communicating." He listened closely to be sure there were two. He was not yet aware of my "double feline" experiences of the day and his story became the third astonishing symbolic synchronicity.

The miraculous nature of synchronicity is part of the ineffable magic of the Universe. That the two events--the Aker symbol's appearance in my life "yesterday" --and this image that arrived "tomorrow" is a great gift. For me this occurrence is as powerful as the golden scarab story told at the beginning of this chapter. In this numinous moment I chose to interpret the symbols that I was on the right track with my writing and that it is worth the time to understand the deeper meaning. "Just trust and do the work," my inner voice seemed to counsel.

As a result of these experiences I was also powerfully reminded that many years ago I had a dream where I walked on a long path that led to the temple of Osiris at Abydos in Egypt, carrying an alabaster jar. Since that time, I have visited Egypt thirteen times. In the dream, as I neared the portal of the temple, there were two large upright white lions on either side of the entrance. They stood as guardians—one male and one female. They were living creatures of rare intelligence with bright blue penetrating eyes. That dream experience has never faded and the presence of those lions has remained with me.

I believe that we can invite golden scarabs, or other powerful symbols, into our lives and learn to discern the meaning and receive gifts of wisdom offered. As we open to the magical nature of Reality our own miracles increase. These symbols and synchronicities can penetrate the force field of our crystalized mental patterns, wounds, and beliefs. When mental barriers of arrogance and fear are overcome, real growth can begin.

We'll begin the journey of discovery by looking back in time to understand the rich legacy of oracles, guides, and dreamwork that has flowed through time. Then we will rediscover the path of our unfolding spiritual nature that beckons.

CHAPTER TWO

Ancient Oracles & Dream Temples

The Wisdom of the Sphinx:
To know, to will, to dare, and to keep silent

The path of ancient wisdom traditions can be traced by looking back in time and following winding footprints of seers and sages left by those who walked this way before. Their steps lead through forests of confusion into the increasing light of understanding.

Seeking guidance through signs, symbols, oracles, and seers is a practice as old as humankind. In ancient times oracles existed at sacred sites around the ancient world where pilgrims traveled, seeking dream interpretation, healing, or guidance in major life decisions. A pilgrimage is a journey to a holy place for a sacred reason. In antiquity a pilgrimage was a major undertaking, often potentially dangerous, and requiring considerable investment of time and resource.

In ancient times people traveled to these sacred places of power, healing temples, and oracle centers, seeking answers. Supplicants were "called" or guided, motivated by some deeply felt need, to undertake the long and sometimes arduous journey to consult the Oracle. These pilgrimages were undertaken at considerable sacrifice and usually only once in a lifetime. People traveled great distances, enduring hardships we can only imagine, and with considerable investment of resources. They often prepared for years and were dedicated to getting the most from their journey. It's likely they carried strong intentions as they journeyed, and a great deal may have been at stake in terms of how they implemented the answers they received.

Oracles

The word oracle is derived from the Latin verb *orare*, which means "to speak." In ancient times an oracle could be a person who was a prophet or wise counselor through whom a certain deity was believed to speak. The oracle was also thought to be the response, message, or revelation itself, given through a prophet in the form of a wise statement or prediction. An oracle was also the shrine or temple consecrated to the worship of a certain prophetic deity where such guidance was sought.

Oracles and seers in ancient Egypt and Greece practiced what we call divination, from the Latin *divinare*, meaning "to foresee, or to be inspired by a deity." And of course, modern oracles and seers still offer wise council in different forms. Oracles were thought to be "portals" through which the gods spoke directly. In this sense they were seen as different from seers who interpreted signs and omens sent by the gods through bird signs, animal entrails, or various other methods.

Omens were sometimes perceived and interpreted by tracking strange and natural phenomena. Augury is a practice from ancient Rome of interpreting omens or signs from observing the behavior of birds. When the individual, who was called an augur, interpreted these signs, this was called "taking the auspices." Auspices is from the Latin *auspicium* and *auspex*, which literally means "one who looks at birds."

This type of omen reading was already more than a thousand years old at the time of Classical Greece. In the 14th century BCE diplomatic correspondence preserved in Egypt, called the *Armana Correspondence*, shows the practice was familiar to the king of Alasia in Cyprus, who requested that an eagle diviner be sent from Egypt.

Oracles were conduits for gods on earth and their prophecies were believed to be the verbatim will of the gods. Because of high demand for oracle consultations, and the oracles' limited work schedules, they were not the main source of divination for the ancient Greeks. That role often fell to the seer. Seers were not in direct contact with the gods, rather they interpreted the signs provided. Seers used many methods to discern the will of the gods, including *extispicy*, which examined animal entrails. Seers were more numerous than oracles, and did not keep a limited schedule, so they were highly valued by all Greeks, not just those with the capacity to travel to Delphi or other distant sites.

Oracular traditions in ancient Egypt reach far back in time. There was a famous oracular site at the renowned temple of the cobra goddess Wadjet at her temple in the Nile Delta, which the Greeks called Buto. The temple is now in ruins but was majestic 5,000 years ago. The cobra on pharaoh's crown was the symbol of Wadjet and held serpent energy, kundalini in Sanskrit. When Egypt was united as one country Wadjet was the symbol of lower Egypt in the north that included the Delta.

Given the parallel between the cobra and python goddesses at these oracle centers (see Delphi below) it is likely that Wadjet's oracle was the earlier source of the tradition that spread from Egypt to Greece like much of Egypt's ancient wisdom. An annual festival called the Going Forth of Wadjet was celebrated on December 25, when the Sun turns each year and begins its journey north. Typical of Egyptian festivals the event included songs, chants, and dance, welcoming the return of the light.

The Oracle of Amun at the Siwa Oasis in western Egypt was made famous when Alexander the Great visited after delivering Egypt from Persian rule in 332 BCE. The ruins are still a popular tourist attraction. Ancient Egyptians traveled to the oracles to ask questions of gods at their annual festivals at different temples—Herodotus is quoted as saying the Oracle of Amun was very reliable.

Delphi, on the slopes of Mount Parnassus in ancient Greece, was perhaps the most famous oracular site of that time. The omphalos stone that was placed there was said to mark the center, or navel, of the Earth. The oracle temple at Delphi was originally the domain of the goddess Gaia, the great earth mother, until patriarchal times when the site and its priestesses were taken over by the priests of the sun god Apollo. In antiquity these sites were always adjacent to a sacred spring and it was always priestesses who performed the work. The oracle priestesses were called Pythia, from Python, who was a giant dragon that the goddess Gaia put at Delphi to guard the sacred shrine. Earliest myths say the *Pythia* were the goddesses Themis and Phoebe and that the site was sacred to Gaia from the most ancient of times, protected by two guardian serpents.

As noted above, the symbolic link between the Greek python and the Egyptian cobra is compelling. When the priests of Apollo took over the shrine thousands of years later, they symbolically destroyed the Python in a similar way that St. George killed the dragon, effectively driving feminine wisdom underground. Apollo replaced the serpent energy with Zeus's solar eagles.

Supplicants who arrived at the oracular site would be led into the temple to enter the *adyton*, the "holy of holies," to put their questions to the Pythia, the oracle priestess. The degree of preparation helped ensure that the supplicant was in a deeply reverent, receptive, and meditative state, similar to the shamanic journey. After they received their answers they would depart.

The *Pythia* sat on tripods with serpent legs that were lodged in underground caves where trance-inducing fumes seeped out of fissures in the rocks. Here, the oracle priestesses uttered their prophecies. Stories say that the priestesses breathed deeply of the mind-altering scent, and entered into an altered state. They were said to speak in a strange tongue, although earlier reports before the takeover of the priests of Apollo, insisted that their messages were clear. However, like our own dream messages or synchronous experiences, what was received from the oracles was often symbolic, even allegorical.

Other important oracles of Greek antiquity were the oracle of Dione and Zeus in Epirus. Epidaurus was another famous center. Other oracles of Apollo were located at Didyma and Mallus on the coast of Anatolia, at Corinth in the Peloponnese, and the islands of Delos and Aegina in the Aegean Sea. The Sibylline Oracles are a collection of oracular utterances written in Greek hexameters and ascribed to the Sibyls, prophetesses who uttered divine revelations in trance states. Fourteen books and eight fragments of Sibylline Oracles survive.

In a testament to the enduring power of these ancient oracles, there is a modern and ancestral African tradition of python priestesses called *Amengansie*. These women are called "black doves," but in more ancient times were also called Sisters of Isis and Sibyls. They worked with a "sacred serpent" and have a living tradition. Tradition holds that they were sometimes sold as slaves but also worked as oracles at Egyptian temples. They have been severely persecuted but their secret tradition still lives on, keeping the link unbroken.

Dreamers through time

Heeding the messages in dreams stretches back in time at least six thousand years—likely much longer. Three thousand years ago the *Upanishads*, Hindu sacred texts, described dreaming as a higher state of consciousness than the waking state. Indigenous shamans around the world consider dreams to be important messages from the spirit world. These native healers and teachers learn to interpret dream symbols, clarifying and illuminating the spiritual lives of their communities.

Australian Aborigines refer to the Dreamtime, or the Dreaming, as a sacred state where the Soul journeys in heavenly realms. Through concentration and breathing Aboriginal shamans claim to enter Dreamtime at will, performing consciously in this state while awake. The Dreaming represents Aboriginal concepts of "everywhen," during which time the land was inhabited by ancestral figures, often of heroic proportions, or with supernatural abilities. These figures were often distinct from deities as they did not control the material world and were not worshipped but only revered. The concept of the Dreamtime has become part of global popular culture.

In her book, *Earth Medicine: Ancestors Ways of Harmony for Many Moons*, Jamie Sams, a member of the Wolf Clan Teaching Lodge, who has ancestors from the Cherokee, Seneca, Choctaw, and Mohawk tribes says, "In ancient times, our people had Dreamers who were honored members of the Tribe because of their abilities of seeing. The Dreamers could access the needs of their Tribe and envision the successful outcomes of the hunt, harvest, or journey. The Clan Mother who is Guardian of the Dreamers, Seers, and Oracles is Looks Far Woman."

Tibetans have a long tradition of working with symbolic dream messages. Tibetan Bon faith healers, who were ancient shamans, used dreams to read the relationship between spirits and humans, and to diagnose diseases. Bon was the very early belief system of Tibet's indigenous people before Buddhism arrived from India. There were also independent female "dream tellers" who served as court psychics. The practice of dream yoga has been used in Tibet since ancient times and is considered an important aspect of medical analysis and mind training.

Chuang Tzu, a Taoist seer, wondered with Shakespeare, if "all life was but a dream." Assurbanipal, an Assyrian king from the seventh century BCE, considered dream elements to be like ciphers, symbols with distinct meaning. Poignant accounts have been shared of loved ones who paused by a dreamer's bedside to say farewell, appearing in a dream at what would later be revealed to be the moment of death. These nighttime visitations are of great comfort to those losing a loved one, supporting the belief that life continues beyond physical form. Dreams also serve as a window to the other side where living people believe to have seen the activities of the deceased through their dreams.

Numerous anecdotes relate how scientists searching for the answer to a problem, writers seeking a plot element, composers searching for the perfect chord, and artists questing for an image, all claim to have received answers in dreams. Albert Einstein said he received dream guidance when he was pondering a difficult mathematical equation. Physicist Neils Bohr saw the model for the atom in a dream. Physicist

Dimitri Mendeleev was working with the 56 elements known at the time when he fell asleep after an exhausting day. He reported, "I saw in a dream a table where all the elements fell into place as required. Awakening, I immediately wrote it down on a piece of paper." He named his discovery the "periodic table of the elements," which we still use.

Author Robert Louis Stevenson received the idea of *The Strange Case of Dr. Jekyll and Mr. Hyde* in a dream, and poet Samuel Taylor Coleridge wrote his poem, *Kubla Khan*, word-for-word as remembered from a dream. As he was recording line 54 someone knocked at his door. He answered, and when he returned to his transcription, regrettably the rest of the poem was lost to him. This story illustrates the importance of capturing dreams immediately upon waking as their presence can be fleeting.

Beneath the paws of the Great Sphinx of Egypt is a stone monument called the stela of the dream. This relic is dated to the time of King Tutmosis IV, a New Kingdom Pharaoh, who ruled nearly 2,500 years ago. When Tutmosis was a young boy the Sphinx was covered to its neck with sand. One day, in the heat of the desert afternoon, the young prince slept in the shadow of the huge head and had a riveting dream. The Sphinx spoke to Tutmosis saying, "Son, cast your eyes upon me. Can you see how long I have been neglected? Deliver me from the sands of ages, and I will crown you king of Upper and Lower Egypt."

Compelled by the voice in his dream, when he woke the prince ordered workers to free the massive statue from the tons of sand surrounding its enormous body. As the voice in the dream had promised Tutmosis was soon crowned Pharaoh. He had the stela inscribed and placed between the leonine paws of the Great Sphinx where the stone remains today.

Another story from Egypt is of Joseph of the coat of many colors. After his brothers sold him into slavery Joseph ended up in Pharaoh's jail where he established a reputation for interpreting dreams. One night, Pharaoh dreamed of seven fat cows entering the Nile, emerging as seven lean cows. Joseph interpreted the dream as a warning that seven years of plenty would be followed by seven years of famine, and counseled the king to take heed and fill the larders. (Genesis 41:17-27) The pharaoh followed Joseph's advice and he rose to the important position of advisor to pharaoh.

Another well-known dream story from the Bible is that of a different Joseph, Mary's husband and earthly father of Jesus, who received a dream warning of danger to his family. He listened to the angel's nighttime summons (Matthew 2:13) and fled to Egypt with his family, saving Jesus from almost certain death at the hands of Herod's executioners. The book of the Bible known as *The Revelation,* or *Apocalypse of Saint John,* was received and transcribed on the Greek island of Patmos. This vision is usually rendered as a dream, which is perhaps the most often interpreted, or misinterpreted, dream on record.

Renowned Virginia Beach psychic Edgar Cayce, who was known as the "sleeping prophet," interpreted dreams while in trance. He paid as much attention to his dreams as his psychic visions and advised others to heed their dreams and invest time learning their language. In one of his trance readings Cayce remarked,". . . dreams are given for the benefit of the individual, would (he or she) but interpret them correctly." (Reading #294-15). Echoing the premise of this book, Edgar Cayce also said that "The dreams . . . come to individuals through the subjugation of the conscious mind, and the subconscious being of the Soul – when loosed -- is able to communicate with the subconscious minds of those whether in the material or the cosmic plane." (Reading #243-5).

Temples of Asklepius

Healing temples called *Asklepions* existed in ancient Greece and in the wider Hellenistic and Roman worlds. The temples were dedicated to Asclepius, son of the god Apollo, who was said to be such an extraordinary healer he could raise the dead. Pilgrims flocked to his temples to seek spiritual and physical healing--and to have dreams.

Two steps were required for a patient to be considered for treatment at an Asklepion temple.

Preparation – preliminary treatment for admission was called *Katharsis*, or "purification," purifying baths and cleansing diets that lasted several days. Other procedures included detoxing the emotions through art. Patients made offerings of money or gifts. The priest of the temple gave the seeker a special prayer to ease the patient's mind and create a more positive outlook for the experience.

Incubation – The next stage was *incubatio*, "incubation," dream therapy, or temple sleep. Patients slept in a dormitory located in the healing temple where they were lulled into a hypnotic state, likely induced by hallucinogens. They began their dream journey with the expectation that they would be visited in their dream by Asclepius himself, or one of his daughters, Hygeia or Panacea. Asclepius also had totem animals in whose guise he might appear to the supplicants as they slept—dog, rooster, and of course, the serpent.

These dream visitations were prognostic and revealed the projected course of the disease and ultimate outcomes. Once awake, patients recounted their dreams to temple priests, who prescribed treatment based on their interpretation of the dream messages. Other dreams were more symbolic. The priests were master dream interpreters who would divine the treatment from the patient's account of the dream. Numerous written accounts provided detailed reports of their cures that attest to patients' healing.

Dream Temple of Delphi

Like the *Asklepion* healing temples, an important part of the work of the famous oracle centers at Delphi was dream interpretation. Delphi in Greece was the most famous oracular site where seekers also came to sleep, perchance to dream, and receive guidance. The famous maxim, "Know Thyself" was carved above the entrance. Two lesser known maxims also appeared in the same location, "Nothing in excess," and "Surety brings ruin." We might understand these maxims as advising insight, exercising discipline, and having humility, which are qualities that help with spiritual work and give strength on the Path.

Our spiritual growth is a process of surrender and metamorphosis. What has to "die" in order for the radiant Phoenix of our unfolding selves to emerge?

Admission was not guaranteed; pilgrims were interviewed by priests or priestesses in preparation for dream work or presentation to the Oracle. Genuine and sincere cases were sorted from the frivolous, and pilgrims went through rituals of purification and exercises to frame their questions. They brought gifts to the oracle in exchange for her answer. Once accepted and prepared they proceeded to the temple in procession along the Sacred Way, carrying laurel leaves, which were symbolic of their pilgrimage.

Once in residence at the dream temple, seekers were instructed how to facilitate a powerful dream. Special techniques were employed to trigger significant guidance dreams. Like the *Asklepion* healing temples seekers were instructed in rites of purification, which included bathing, oils, herbs, and a special purifying diet. Most importantly, they were taught to ask for the dream, and how to frame the question, to receive wise counsel.

The counsel and dream interpretation given by the oracle or temple priestesses was meant to shape choices and future action. Having come a long way at great cost aspirants were in a mood to listen. The nature of a dream and its meaning were considered with far reaching implications. Sometimes the fate of nations, and the possibility of war, was at stake.

Egyptian Dream Temples

In ancient Egypt, priests also acted as dream interpreters at temple oracle centers. Dreams were considered to be divine messages that held predictions for the future. *The Ancient Egyptian Book of Dreams* is the oldest known manual of dream interpretation. The Egyptian dream book is a papyrus with a hieratic (priestly) cursive script that was found in the ancient Egyptian workers' village of Deir el-Medina, near the Valley of the Kings, in the library of the scribe Kenhirkhopeshef.

The papyrus was already old in his time. Dated to the early reign of Ramesses II (1279-1213 BCE) the dream book contains 108 dreams, describing 78 activities and emotions. The Dream Book was part of an archive, including a wide variety of literary, magical, and documentary material, which was an heirloom passed down through the family for more than a century. The papyrus currently resides at the British Museum and lists a number of dreams and their interpretations.

The activities described experiences of the average person in ordinary life. Most dealt with some form of seeing. The second largest category related to eating and drinking, and a few discussed intimate relations. The papyrus pages have vertical columns of hieratic signs that began: "if a man sees himself in a dream…" The text first lists good dreams, and then bad; the word "bad" is written in red, which was considered the color of ill omen. Dreaming of a deep well-meant prison while a mirror indicated a second wife. A shining moon was associated with forgiveness, and a large cat symbolized a bumper crop. Looking out of a window was good as it meant the gods could hear his cry.

The Great Sphinx of Egypt is much older than conventional Egyptology claims based on geological research and the pattern of weathering. I believe the original form may have been a female lion—most Egyptian feline deities were feminine. Other evidence suggests that the head was re-carved as it is now much smaller in proportion to the body. One of the earliest and most powerful Egyptian deities was the feline goddess Mafdet, who appears on beds and chairs that now reside in museums. She was a goddess of justice who was also was a fierce protector of pharaoh.

The great Sphinx of Giza was considered to be a guardian and the treasure that was guarded was hidden knowledge. The Sphinx faces due east and is therefore a seasonal marker of the equinoxes as the Sun rises and sets due east and west at spring and fall equinoxes. In myth and occult symbolism, the Sphinx was said to be a fourfold creature with the forebody of lion, the wings of eagle, a human face, and the back body of a bull and to represent what is called the "wisdom of the Sphinx" quoted at the beginning of this chapter—to know, to will, to dare, and to keep silent. The wisdom of this combined creature was therefore said to represent the four fixed signs of the Zodiac:

To know	Human-Aquarius
To will	Bull-Taurus
To dare	Lion-Leo
To keep silent	Eagle-Scorpio

Like sphinxes, dragons were also thought to guard treasure, especially gold, which is a symbol of wisdom and mastery in alchemy. Dragon comes from the Greek *drakon*, which means "watcher," a type of guardian. Although dragons are often portrayed as dangerous creatures who breathe fire, in the mythology of Asia, they are always seen as wise and beneficent beings. In fact, the dynasty of emperors is believed to be descended from dragons who mated with human women.

There is also a sphinx creature called a *lamma* in Sumerian iconography. Considered to be a protective deity the lamma was often placed at thresholds. Knowing the secret password to enter is implied in their guardian function. In earliest times the *lamma* was female, but in later Assyrian times it became a hybrid of human, bird, bull and/or lion with a human head. In this form it was call *lamassu*.

In Greek myth, the sphinx was a female monster with the same fourfold aspect. The famous riddle of the Sphinx in Greek myth relates that she devoured travelers who could not answer her question: "What creature walks on four legs in the morning, two legs at noon, and three in the evening?" The hero Oedipus gave the correct answer, "man," representing a human lifetime, where in the morning of our lives as infants we crawl on four "legs," walk upright on two legs as an adult in mid-life or noon, and symbolically use a cane as a third leg in old age, or the evening of our lives. Giving the right answer caused the sphinx's death and gave Oedipus the ability to continue his heroic journey.

✿ ✿ ✿

The dynamic of an oracle has to do with receptivity, and when we seek counsel we have to be open to receive. When we learn to view dreams and synchronicities as our own personal oracles the guidance we receive can be profound. We have to put ourselves in an appropriate frame of mind that includes maintaining a positive attitude with the expectation that we will receive the guidance we've requested.

Oracles and dream temples no longer exist; instead, we have psychiatry, with the use of drugs to augment talk therapy, and psychological counseling. Neither of these disciplines focuses on a spiritual quest. We might ask if dreams still have value in the modern world. Can science and modern research give insight?

CHAPTER THREE

What Science Says

Dreams help regulate traffic on that fragile bridge
that connects our experiences with our emotions and memories.

~ Sander van der Linden PhD, *Scientific American*

Current research into sleep and dreams sheds light on why we should pay attention to ancient traditions and bring the testimony of ages into the modern world, even if only for the sake of our health. The latest evidence indicates that sleep and dreams are more important than ever in a world filled with stress and overwhelming input. The ancients may have placed value on dreams mostly for guidance, but science is revealing that our very lives are at stake without adequate sleep and dreaming.

The brain makes up only about 2% of the body's weight but uses 20%, or ten times that amount, of the body's energy. Our brains work in a similar manner to computers, receiving data from our senses and body, processing this information and sending messages back to the body through the nervous system, a network that controls the body's functions. Brain tissue is composed of nearly 100 billion neurons and an astonishing trillion stabilizing cells.

There is good reason we don't remember the millions of stimuli our brains receive and process every day. Scientists estimate that we have 60,000 thoughts every day. Processing this inundation would be counterproductive, not to mention overwhelming. There's a mechanism in our brain-consciousness called the Reticular Activating System, RAS, that sorts stimuli that merit remembering based on criteria of their potential threat or likely benefit. This mechanism allows us to focus on what seems important and allows literally millions of data points to be ignored by our conscious minds. I have a theory that the RAS gets more selective with age and may impact short term memory loss.

We can override this sorting mechanism in specific instances. For example, as you go about your daily routine you may pass dozens of white cars. Unless there is something unusual or striking, you don't notice. If someone tells you that tomorrow you will receive one hundred dollars for every white car you see, suddenly they pop up everywhere. We can "train" our minds to pay attention by suggesting that this stimulus is now important. This is the potential benefit of working consciously with the RAS.

The human brain is divided into two hemispheres. The left hemisphere is considered the "logical brain," and is involved in language and analysis, and the right hemisphere is usually described as the "creative brain," involved in imagination and creative expression. Emotion is the domain of the right brain in both humans and non-human primates. The left hemisphere controls the right side of the body while the right hemisphere controls the left side. The left brain is more active in speech production than the right. In most people, the two main language areas, known as Broca's area and Wernicke's area, are found in the left hemisphere. People who are deaf show speech-like brain activity when watching sign language.

The left and right sides of the brain are connected by a large number of nerve fibers. Dr. Ananya Mandal states, "In a healthy brain, the two sides send constant signals back and forth. Unless the connection between the right and left brain is physically severed, information zips across the hemispheres every second during most of the tasks our brains accomplish."

Recent brain imaging studies have shown no differences between men and women in brain lateralization. However, the side of the brain, or hemisphere, used in each activity is not the same for every person and may be influenced by whether a person is left or right-handed. Contributions towards this 'brain lateralization' research won Roger W. Sperry the Nobel Prize in 1960. Popular cultural exaggeration of these findings led to unfortunate stereotypical beliefs about left brain and right brain personalities.

Two Hemispheres of the Brain

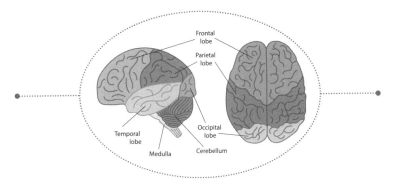

Anatomically the brain is also divided into several lobes:

- Frontal lobes are responsible for problem solving, judgment, and motor function
- Parietal lobes manage sensation, handwriting, and body position
- Temporal lobes are involved with memory and hearing
- Occipital lobes contain the brain's visual processing system

As part of the Central Nervous System, our brains emit what science calls "brain waves," synchronized electrical impulses that oscillate in wave patterns from the neurons in our brain and are detected through EEGs, electroencephalography. Brain waves are associated with different levels of awareness, ranging from hyper-alertness to deep and dreamless sleep. Science has identified five brain waves that operate simultaneously, although one is dominant at any given time depending on our activity.

The waves are measured in Hertz, which is a unit of frequency in the International System of Units (SI) defined as one cycle per second.

Hertz is named after the German physicist Heinrich Rudolf Hertz, the first person to provide conclusive proof of the existence of electromagnetic waves. Brain waves are synchronized electrical pulses that are produced when neurons in your brain communicate with each other. Different brain waves are produced by thoughts, emotions, and behavior and differ according to your mood and activity. Slower brain waves are dominant when you feel tired and brain waves of higher frequency indicate alertness. Although all brain waves are present at all times, one frequency is usually dominant, depending on our activity or state of mind.

The five brain waves are:

Beta (12-30 Hz) waves are dominant in normal waking consciousness and are heightened during times of stress. When Beta waves are dominant the focus of the mind is external. Beta waves indicate focused concentration and are present during conversations and decision making where mental alertness is important. Beta waves are believed to increase logical thinking.

Alpha (7.5-14 Hz) waves appear primary in relaxation but while we remain awake. This level is thought to generate creativity and to help in problem solving. Alpha waves are also associated with meditation and increase in the posterior part of the brain. Alpha waves calm the nervous system, lower blood pressure and heart rate, and reduce production of stress hormones.

Theta (4-7.5 Hz) waves relate to deep relaxation and meditative states, hypnosis, trance, and light sleep and are associated with dreaming. In the theta state the senses are withdrawn from the external world and the focus is inward. Theta waves are believed to enhance positive mental states.

Delta (0.5-4 Hz) waves have the slowest frequency and are primary in deep and dreamless sleep. Delta waves increase the production of two anti-aging hormones, DHEA and melatonin. Delta waves facilitate healing as this deep state allows the body to release toxins that built up during the day.

Gamma (above 40 Hz) waves are the fastest and the least recognized or understood but are thought to be associated with intense concentration, sudden insight, and high levels of awareness and information processing. Gamma waves decrease anxiety and increase positive emotions.

Brain waves also seem to be associated with different parts of the brain. For example, alpha waves are strongest at the back of the brain in the occipital lobe that handles vision. The optimal level for visualization is the Alpha-Theta border at 7-8 Hz, which is believed to be the gateway to the subconscious mind. Some researchers believe that gamma waves equate to the highest level of cognitive function and are like the Buddhist idea of being "awake." Most people experience this briefly as a eureka moment of insight and euphoria, but Buddhist monks or nuns may be in this state for long periods during meditation. This may be the state where the startling impact of a synchronicity occurs.

Hypnosis

Hypnosis is a trance state that is characterized by focused attention, concentration, reduced peripheral awareness, and an enhanced capacity to respond to suggestion. Ironically, the word comes from the Greek *hypnos*, which means sleep. There are competing theories to explain hypnosis and related phenomena. What are termed "altered state" theories see hypnosis as an altered state of mind that is different from ordinary awareness, while other theories consider hypnosis to be a type of "dissociative" state. I will explore the wider subject of consciousness in Chapter Five.

Hypnosis is typically a cooperative interaction between a responsive participant and a suggestive hypnotist. A session usually begins with an induction that involves a series of preliminary instructions and suggestions. People in a hypnotic state may appear sleepy or "zoned out," but are instead in a state of hyper-awareness. In this state, the body is deeply relaxed and brain waves are in the alpha-theta border, from 7Hz to 8 Hz, which is considered to be the optimal range for visualization, suggestion, intention, and creativity. Hypnosis, or hypnotherapy, is now used to help with pain control in cancer patients, sleep disorders and insomnia, smoking cessation, over eating, migraines, anxiety, post-traumatic stress, and the pain of childbirth.

Another valuable use of hypnosis is the technique called regression, and past-life regression, which examines and works to heal memories from early experiences in this lifetime as well as karma from past lives. I have had considerable personal experience with this aspect of hypnosis, which became the subject of the 5-Star series of books written with my husband Ted Denmark, PhD, that are based on my own trance experiences. The topic of regression will be covered in some detail in Chapter 6 where I discuss the body of trance work of Edgar Cayce and Dr. Michael Newton. (See the Resource section at the back of this book).

Meditation

Meditation is also a trance state, most often self-induced, where a person uses a technique such as focusing on an object, like a candle, or a thought to focus awareness. Brain waves are in the same range in hypnosis and meditation, and while the states similar, they are not the same. The earliest records of meditation are found in the Vedas, ancient Hindu texts. Meditation techniques have been shown to reduce stress, anxiety, depression, and pain. On the even more positive side, meditation can enhance a sense of peace and well-being. Current research is examining the effect on psychological and physical health.

We might ask if meditation is a form of hypnosis, or if hypnosis is a form of meditation. In current practice hypnosis is generally facilitated by a trained practitioner, while meditation is more commonly a solitary pursuit. However, people practice self-hypnosis and sit in groups to experience guided meditation. These are states of mind and consciousness that are still not fully understood.

Sleep

Sleep is a dynamic and complex process that science is just beginning to understand. We spend roughly a third of our life asleep, and two hours every night dreaming. If we spend that much time sleeping and dreaming these activities must be highly significant to our wellbeing. Neurotransmitters, nerve-signaling chemicals, turn off as we become sleepy, and chemicals that keep the brain active while we are awake, like norepinephrine and orexin, subside. Other chemicals that balance sleep and alertness interact to shift us from wakefulness to sleep. As noted above, most sleeping is characterized by Delta brain waves, the large slow waves where muscles are relaxed and breathing is slow and deep. This deeps state of relaxation aids the brain and body to recuperate and recharge.

Research at the National Institute of Neurological Disorders has shown that quality sleep is as important as food and water as sleep impacts a number of brain functions. The brain and body are quite active during sleep. Recent studies show that sleep removes toxins that build up in the body when we are awake, reenergizing the body's cells, and supporting learning and memory. Sleep clears waste from the brain and also affects all the tissues and organs in the body, repairing tissues and growing bones. Research shows that chronic lack of sleep increases the risk of high blood pressure, heart disease, diabetes, obesity, and depression. Sleep needs vary by age and among individuals. Newborns need as much as fifteen hours while some adults seem able to thrive on seven.

Sleep is not uniform. Instead, over the course of the night, total sleep is made up of several rounds of the sleep cycle, which is composed of four individual stages. In a typical night, we go through four to six sleep cycles that repeat over the course of the night. Not all cycles are the same length, but average about 90 minutes each. Each cycle has five stages:

> ***Stage One*** – Usually lasts a few minutes and is non-REM (Rapid Eye Movement) sleep when we first fall asleep. Heart rate and breathing slow. Muscles start to relax and alpha and theta brain waves are dominant.

Stage Two – Lasts about 25 minutes. Body temperature drops and heart rate and breathing slow further. No eye movements occur during this stage.

Stages Three & Four – Non-REM sleep where the body is deeply relaxed. Delta brain waves are dominant in this stage while tissues repair, cells regenerate, and the immune system strengthens.

Stage Five – REM stage occurs at about 90 minutes after falling asleep and lasts about 60 minutes. The so-called dreaming stage of sleep is characterized by Rapid Eye Movements—REM. Limbs become paralyzed and heart rate and breathing increase. Brain activity greatly increases in this main dreaming stage.

Adequate rest allows the body to produce sufficient amounts of cytokines, a protein produced during sleep that targets infection and inflammation and strengthens the immune response. While sleeping the body sends fluids to organs and tissues, replenishing cells and removing excess fluid from other areas. Collagen is also produced during sleep, which helps promote smoother skin and prevents dark circles under the eyes, reducing wrinkles and fine lines.

Sleep deprivation studies have shown how essential both sleep and dreaming are to our mental and emotional wellbeing. Research subjects who were wakened during dreams, and were unable to continue processing, developed anxiety, emotional upsets, and other temporary disorders in their waking life.

Matthew Walker PhD, is a professor of psychology and neuroscience at the University of California, Berkeley, and director of the university's Center for Human Sleep Science. In his bestselling book, *Why We Sleep: Unlocking the Power of Sleep and Dreams*, Walker says,

> Scientists have known for some time that shorter sleep times are tied to heart disease and stroke. Mounting evidence also indicates that sleep deprivation leads to a higher risk of obesity, diabetes,

depression, and Alzheimer's disease. Sleep helps memory retention and increases our ability and speed in learning facts and skills, making it important for everyone. Large population studies reflect a startling truth—the less you sleep, the shorter your life.

Dr. Walker's research also confirms that "sleep is the single most effective thing we can do to rest our brain and recharge our physical health each day. And above sleep, dreaming provides essential emotional first aid and is a unique form of informational alchemy."

My own work and research indicate that dreams, and synchronicities, are also the keys to our personal growth and spiritual development.

Dreams

Oneirology, from the Greek *oneiron* "dream" and *logia*, is the scientific study of dreams. Oneirology studies the process of dreams quantitatively rather than interpreting meaning. Ironically, logia means "communication of divine origin." Research shows that everyone dreams every night even if we don't remember, and studies have shown that we spend about two hours every night in the dream state, whether or not we recall our dreams. Most dreams last from 5-20 minutes. Some people dream in color, while others seem to recall only black and white dream images.

Research also suggests that most dream activity occurs in the final hour of sleep, acting like a recap of the night's dream sequences and overnight processing. So, planning for a good night's rest can be a vital component in the process of recalling our dreams. The common adages "sleep on it," and "sleep tight" may have much more significance than we thought. B vitamins have also been shown to improve dream retention because of their relationship to mental functioning and nerve health. B vitamins seem to play a role in memory storage and dream recall, so increasing intake of these nutrients may improve retention.

Dreams as a part of the overall sleep experience also seem to serve an important function in learning and healing. New born babies experience the most intense and longest duration of REM sleep. Researchers believe this may be related to the rate of growth and development and amount of learning that occurs at this early stage of life.

✿   ✿   ✿

Shifting now from science, which is just beginning to realize the vital importance of dreams, to what we will call sacred science, we will explore knowledge from ancient traditions that reveals what modern science has lost. We will learn how much that has been hidden or veiled can help us gain a deeper understanding of our Soul's purpose.

CHAPTER FOUR

Sacred Science: Alchemy & Esoteric Anatomy

You are not a drop of water in the ocean;
you are the entire ocean in the drop.

~ Jalāl ad-Dīn Muhammad Rumi

Science has revealed a great deal about our physical anatomy, but are there more layers to this knowledge that conceal deeper wisdom? Learning about alchemy, and the plan that is encoded within its chemical symbolism, is a good place to begin. The ancient land of Egypt called me from early childhood, and I have returned a dozen times. At its height before the pandemic, upwards of ten million tourists visited Egypt every year. I believe we sense the profound mysteries that were known in the temples of ancient Egypt, and we long to bring this magic back into our lives.

The word chemistry derives from alchemy, which in turn comes from the Arabic word al *kimiya*. According to diverse sources *al kimiya* came from the ancient name of Egypt, *Khem*, which meant "black," describing the rich dark soil bordering the Nile River. Scholars believe this also carries the memory of hidden ancient wisdom that came out of Egypt as Islamic scholars carried the knowledge of alchemy into the Middle Ages.

Alchemy was the precursor of chemistry and was based on the supposed transmutation of base metals into gold, or to find a universal elixir for this purpose. Gold was the quest of the alchemists and the ancient Egyptians used the precious metal in abundance. According to Greek historians, Egyptian mysteries that included alchemy came from the legendary Egyptian figure Hermes Trismegistus (thrice blessed) four thousand years ago. The knowledge was encoded on what came to be known as the *Emerald Tablets of Thoth*, the Egyptian name of Hermes. This knowledge became known as the *Corpus Hermeticum* and is the basis of a philosophical tradition that went from Egypt to Greece, flowing through time for thousands of years as esoteric knowledge.

Medieval alchemists arranged chemical elements into the first rudimentary periodic tables and introduced distillation to Western Europe. Many sciences emerged from alchemy, including medicine, metallurgy, physics, chemistry, cosmology, and astronomy. In this spiritual tradition what was called the philosopher's stone, *lapis philosophorom* in Latin, is a legendary alchemical substance claimed to be able to turn base metals such as iron, tin, lead, mercury, and copper into gold.

The philosopher's stone was the most sought after goal of alchemy as the stone also acted as an elixir of life with the power to cure illness, restore youth, and even grant immortality to those who possessed this priceless substance. The philosopher's stone may not have been a stone at all but another type of exotic substance that was variously known as the "tincture" or "powder." Efforts to discover the philosopher's stone, and to understand the ongoing spiritual process, was called *Magnum Opus*, the Great Work.

In alchemy, when this was expressed as a series of chemical processes, the work has most often been expressed in seven stages: calcination, dissolution, separation, conjunction, fermentation, distillation, and coagulation. Each of the seven stages has a chemical definition as well as a psycho-spiritual process. Although the seven phases of alchemical transformation are represented in chemical language they also represent stages on the spiritual path. In spiritual alchemy the athanor, from Arabic *al tannoor*, which is a "bread oven," is the symbol of the alchemist, who is the burning ground, as the fires of the furnace burn away the false ego.

Often cited as the first of her kind by Zosimus of Panopolis, Maria the Hebrew, also called Maria Prophetissa, was a famous alchemist. She lived in ancient Egypt around the first century CE and is credited with inventing an alchemical device that copies the process of distillation in nature. Alchemists believed this was the basis for producing gold. Maria's remarkable apparatus became a staple in modern chemistry labs. The *kerotakis* heated substances and collected vapors. The device is an airtight container with a sheet of copper on its upper side. When working properly, all its joints form a tight vacuum.

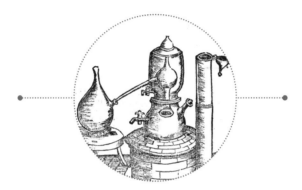

While the traditions of laboratory alchemy have continued into the twentieth and twenty-first centuries, alchemy's symbology and terminology have also greatly enriched efforts to understand the language of the Soul over the past century in part through the work of C. G. Jung. Jung saw what he called the Unconscious as a treasure house of rich imagery and forces he called "Archetypes" that could awaken the life of the Soul. His perspective was informed by his own rich soul life, and by his study of the literature of the Western Hermetic Tradition.

As mentioned in Chapter One, Dr. Marie-Louise Von Franz authored twenty books on the subjects of Egypt, alchemy, and archetypes among others, and interpreted 65,000 dreams in her clinical work. She translated many alchemical texts for Jung during the long years of their collaboration. Alchemy was a fascination for Dr. Jung and he investigated the psychological processes that were encoded in the chemical terms. In his book *Psychology and Alchemy,* he makes the case for alchemy as a symbol of the psychoanalytical process and explains his theory of universal archetypes, affirming that spirituality is an important component in the psychic health of the modern person.

Dream work is alchemy since, in the truest sense alchemy is art, taking something ordinary and transforming the object into something extraordinary. Spiritual alchemy provides a blueprint of becoming, as I have termed the template elsewhere, and the seven stages of transformation are held in potential in the seven energy centers of what has been called our esoteric or sacred anatomy. As we will see, the pattern of seven appears in many places.

Esoteric Anatomy

Science has given us an excellent understanding of the physical anatomy and biology of our brain and body, and how the systems of the body work, some of which was discussed in Chapter Three. The endocrine system and glands trigger our biological maturity through hormone secretion, regulating moods, growth, and reproduction. Our bodies are electro-chemical "machines," but there is an energic aspect that is not apparent (usually) to the senses and which is key to understanding the wisdom encoded in spiritual alchemy and other spiritual traditions.

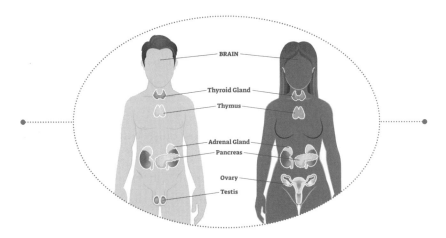

Although this knowledge was essentially lost, or went underground in the west until recently, due to persecution from religion and academia, there is a plan, a sort of course curriculum, that shows the steps along the path. This plan for our spiritual development is within us, held in potential in our esoteric anatomy, but it is consciousness and our awakening awareness that drive the unfolding process. We are meant to become keepers of the sacred flame, but unlike biological maturation, our spiritual development requires our conscious participation. How does our consciousness aid the process?

Western science does not address what has been called our esoteric anatomy, which is known in the Ayurveda system in the east, Chinese acupuncture system, the Hermetic tradition, and in diverse indigenous cultures. The endocrine glands pictured opposite are the outward physical expression of what are called *chakras* in Sanskrit, spinning energetic "wheels" that are related to our spiritual maturity. These centers are located along the spine (not on the front of the body as illustrations like the one below suggests) as invisible "force fields" that power the glands.

The seven main centers form an electromagnetic field along the spine, operating in a particular frequency range. Each field creates a clockwise circular motion of energy. These spinning wheels of energy, sometimes described as "spheres of fire," correspond to certain nerve bundles, major organs, and the endocrine glands. In Ayurveda, and various Yoga traditions such as Tantra and Kundalini, the *chakras* are understood to interact with both the physical and energetic bodies as the intermediary between them.

The *chakras* are called "interior stars" in alchemy and are symbolically connected with planets in astrology and the metals to be transformed in alchemy. Dr. Deepak Choprah terms *chakras* "centers of awareness." He describes the solar plexus center (3) as holding power and warrior energy; love at the heart center (4); creativity at the throat (5), insight and higher awareness at the brow (6), and transcendence at the crown (7). The lower centers (1 & 2) relate to survival and procreation respectively. As we grow in spiritual awareness the potential of these energy centers is activated through a reservoir of energy, *Kundalini* in Sanskrit, which is released from a potential state at the base of the spine. It is beyond the scope of this book to describe this in detail, but the process is central to our spiritual development. *Kundalini* is usually translated as "slumbering serpent." Held in potential like a coiled snake, when awakened this serpentine energy rises and coils through the central channel of the spine, *Sushuma* in Sanskrit, spiraling upward through two other channels, *Ida* and *Pingala*, that form a caduceus-like structure. The rising energy activates and "spiritualizes" the *chakras*. Disciplines such a Yoga, meditation, and shifting to a plant-based diet, are helpful in this process.

Physics and Metaphysics – Phenomenology of Consciousness

Some researchers hold that consciousness is a property of matter so fundamental that even an electron is conscious to some extent. Known as Panpsychism, this philosophy believes that mind, or a mindlike aspect, is an intrinsic feature of reality. I would use the word 'consciousness' instead of 'mind.' Panpsychism is one of the oldest philosophical theories and has been ascribed to a variety of philosophers including Thales, Plato, Spinoza, Leibniz, William James, Alfred North Whitehead, Bertrand Russell, and Galen Strawson. The word was coined by Italian philosopher Francesco Patrizi in the sixteenth century and derives from the two Greek words *pan* "all" and psyche "soul or mind."

As we are increasingly becoming aware, leading edge quantum physics seems to confirm certain tenets of ancient wisdom. Everything in the Universe is made up of energy and everything is interconnected. We partake of one great Unity. Ideas such as "non-locality" and "quantum entanglement" assert that everything in the Universe is connected in real time. I believe grasping the significance of this connectivity is key to working with dreams and navigating life more intentionally.

Our growth and advancement are driven by consciousness. Ancient wisdom holds that consciousness is the fundamental nature of reality and the ability to experience and express increasing levels of consciousness is a function of evolution. The Universe itself, the pure plenum of consciousness, expresses along a vast spectrum, and I believe the plan of a Universe is for consciousness to evolve and develop through ever more complex forms. On a grander cosmic scale, but similar to what's encoded in a fertilized human embryo, a Universe carries the potential of vast expansion and expression from the beginning of its existence. Although measured in a span of time unimaginable on a human scale, a Universe is born, grows, ages, and dies.

A butterfly expresses consciousness at a lower level than a cat, and a human expresses a higher level than an animal, but not yet at the level of what are called "masters of wisdom." In the case of minerals, plants, and animals not much development in awareness occurs over the span of one lifetime. In humans however, the plan within our esoteric anatomy that is described above, when recognized and worked with, allows for accelerated development.

As we will explore further in the next chapter, leading edge science is increasingly providing evidence and context that supports tenets of ancient wisdom. We are gaining vocabulary and knowledge from the frontiers of research into consciousness that help us understand what the ancients have known for thousands of years.

Julie Loar

CHAPTER FIVE

Quantum Hologram & Consciousness

When the electron vibrates, the whole universe shakes.

~ Sir Arthur Stanley Eddington, Founder of Quantum Physics

I have come to believe that time, and what we call spatial "reality," are more fluid and linked in multi-dimensional existence than they appear. Presaging modern physics, the ancient Hindus described the goddess Maya as the universal Creatrix and matrix of all manifested reality. She represents the movement of energy in physical reality and wears the garments and cloaks of form. In metaphysics we are accustomed to hearing that the visible world is an "illusion" and that nothing is permanent. This "illusion" of physical reality is not a falsehood merely because it is an appearance. The tangible world of the senses is certainly not only what it seems on the surface, and science tells us that our bodies are made up of atoms that are separated by immense distances.

The current standard science model informs us that the visible Universe, what can be seen and measured, including all the stars and galaxies, is only 5% of what exists. Physicists describe a mysterious and hypothetical "dark matter" and "dark energy" that make up the other 95%. The nature of reality is still very much an enigma to science, and these provisional names only add to the mystery. So-called dark matter is thought to be a form of matter that accounts for approximately 27% of the matter in the Universe and about a quarter of its total energy density.

Dark matter is implied by observations in astrophysics, including gravitational effects that cannot be explained by accepted theories of gravity, unless more matter is present than can be seen. For this reason, experts believe dark matter is abundant and has had a strong influence on the structure and evolution of the Universe. Dark matter is called "dark" because it does not appear to interact with observable light, or electromagnetic radiation, and cannot be detected by existing instruments. Because dark matter has not yet been observed directly—whatever it is—somehow interacts with ordinary matter and radiation through gravity. But we don't really understand gravity either.

Going further down the rabbit hole, physicists describe another enigmatic aspect of reality they term dark energy. This is an unknown form of "energy" that affects the Universe on the largest of scales. Theorized from measurements of supernovae, which showed that the Universe does not expand at a constant rate, but is rather accelerating, scientists theorize that some yet unknown force must be hypothesized to explain why the Universe is actually expanding rather than contracting as was expected. Dark energy makes up approximately 68% of the Universe, and scientists believe this energy is associated with the vacuum of space. Dark energy seems to be distributed evenly throughout the Universe, even though this is still highly speculative in standard science.

Apollo astronaut Edgar Mitchell, ScD, a physicist from the prestigious Massachusetts Institute of Technology, spoke in terms of a quantum hologram. This concept describes a paradoxical reality termed quantum entanglement, a term coined by Nobel Prize winning physicist Erwin Schroedinger. Physicist Albert Einstein called this "spooky action at a distance" and doubted this could be true.

The basic idea of quantum entanglement is that two particles can be intimately linked even if separated by vast distances across space-time. A change occurring in one affects the other. Quantum entanglement occurs when two discrete entities, such as photons, interact energetically and become inextricably linked. Whatever happens to one immediately affects the other--regardless of how far apart they are. ESP, synchronicity, dream guidance, and even miracles may occur in these yet mysterious realms.

Another perplexing mystery is seen in outcomes of early quantum experiments. The result can change depending on whether or not some property of particles involved are measured. This so-called "observer effect" deeply troubled pioneers of quantum theory because it seemed to undermine the basic assumption behind all science--that there is an objective external world out there that exists irrespective of us. I don't believe "out there" exists--we are part of the Universe. Within this universal view everything happens at once, and the awareness of all events is registered in every part of the Universe. The Universe, therefore, cannot be outside of us; we exist within the Cosmos like drops of water in the ocean or snowflakes in a storm. We partake of the totality of the Universe, which is an interconnected web, and when one strand is plucked the whole web vibrates.

Ancient Wisdom traditions have long taught that if we are properly prepared, we can access levels of knowledge that reside in this quantum hologram in what might be thought of as a Cosmic Internet. We can become magnificent search engines, widening our horizons and deepening our own wisdom nature. We must learn to attune ourselves to the frequency, like an Internet URL, to receive the symbolic signals and decode and interpret the revealed meaning. This requires attention, focus, and commitment.

Consciousness

The Greek word *Psyche* is sometimes translated as "soul," and the Greeks used the term to describe the totality of human consciousness. C. G. Jung perceived the Psyche as a three-fold entity composed of conscious, unconscious, and Oversoul. Jung believed the Psyche worked in a similar manner as the physical body does in homeostasis. He believed what he termed the "unconscious" worked to bring the Psyche into equilibrium, using feedback to the conscious mind through dream symbolism and waking synchronicities. He coined the term "matrix of dreams" for the unconscious and stressed the critical importance of paying attention to the messages that arise from dreams. Jung wrote in *Man and His Symbols* that "For the sake of mental stability and physiological health, the unconscious and conscious must be integrally connected and thus move on parallel lines."

In a similar way, and perhaps even with similar proportions to matter and energy as discussed above, our Psyche is composed of what have usually been termed waking consciousness, personal subconsciousness, and a vast reservoir termed collective unconsciousness. A level of awareness sometimes called super-consciousness is thought to be the level of the Soul. Ordinary waking consciousness, like the material world, may only perceive 5% of what exists in our Psyche.

Like the Universe itself, what we are aware of in our ordinary state of mind is but a tiny fraction of all that is. What is called dark matter may be like our subconscious state, and dark energy may be comparable to the vast reservoir of collective unconscious. In the domain beyond our ordinary waking awareness we are in a realm of mystery where simple explanations for precognition, prophetic dreams, synchronicities, and serendipities are the order of the day (or night).

Science and philosophy have yet to understand the deeper nature of consciousness, and the idea that the brain is the source of consciousness still lingers in some circles. Dr. Eben Alexander, MD, author of *Proof of Heaven*, remarked "Individuals who have been brain dead, and miraculously returned to ordinary awareness, had rich experiences while their physical brains were unable to function. Where were they, and how did this happen?"

Physicist Nassim Haramein has likewise remarked, "The brain is the antenna—not the football game."

Without venturing too far into the quantum theory of leading-edge astrophysics, the world of Plancks, quarks, and black holes, we can learn from the brilliant and pioneering research of physicist Nassim

Haramein, who directs the Resonance Science Foundation. According to Ted Denmark, PhD, who is a member of the foundation and studying this material in depth,

> "The research is showing that the surface-to-volume interior structure of the proton, well-known to standard model science, is the starting point for a completely new extension of precise mathematical physics since the modeling concept of close packing of photons into its interior has led to his initial major breakthrough. Correspondingly, photons or light pulsations, Eddington's 'quantum of action' in electromagnetic radiation, Haramein terms 'Planck Units,' describing these as the fundamental units of energy at the mid-level of the universe."

What is now called this Planck Unit was originally proposed by theoretical physicist Max Planck in 1899, who is also credited with founding quantum theory. Denmark further says, "Going to the ultimate fundamental level or depth in his new theory, Haramein further posits that at the sub-photonic, or sub-Planck Unit level, there is an ultimately vanishingly small existence, the unit of consciousness yet formally unnamed by him (but given credence as the "Neutrino," the proposed name for superluminal "particles" earlier in the last century)." This leading edge research aligns with ancient wisdom, suggesting that at its fundamental level, everything in the Universe is linked and driven by a network of consciousness, a kind of Universal Mind.

Dr. Edgar Mitchell theorized that "There is a spectrum of consciousness available to human beings. At one end is material consciousness. At the other end is what we call 'field' consciousness, where a person is at one with the universe." In my understanding, he means if we only perceive what we believe to be "out there," this is the basis for a kind of simplistic "seeing is believing" mindset. This narrow view disconnects us from the true and ultimate nature of reality.

Arthur Eddington also said, "The physical world is entirely abstract and without actuality apart from its linkage to consciousness." I believe he meant that without someone to participate in the physical world and give it meaning, what we call reality would only be dancing particles of light.

The research of Rupert Sheldrake, PhD, *The Presence of the Past: Morphic Resonance and the Habits of Nature,* falls into the same mind-bending realm. Sheldrake's description of morphic resonance suggests that "memory is inherent in nature and that natural systems share a collective memory from all previous things of their kind." This may be similar to Jung's earlier idea of the collective unconscious. Sheldrake proposes that morphic resonance is responsible for "telepathy-type interconnections between organisms." His fascinating research includes stunning examples of animals knowing when their humans were arriving home, regardless of a schedule, and "a sense of being stared at."

In order for consciousness to function on the physical plane there has to be a "solid" material component, which is our brain and body. The expression "body, mind, and spirit" has often been used to describe the full nature of a person. Dr. Deepak Choprah has said, "The body is a network of intelligence in a field of consciousness, and consciousness is the source of mind." We know we have physical anatomy, as well as the esoteric anatomy described earlier, and beyond this we realize that our existence is more than just our bodies. But what is consciousness, and should we also consider an anatomy of consciousness that describes the Psyche?

Psyche

We can think of the Psyche as a trinity and imagine that what we often call "mind," or consciousness, has three main modes of expression. As is being demonstrated by the pioneering research noted above of physicist of Nassim Haramein, the fundamental units of the universe are neutrinos, units of consciousness. The most common threefold descriptions of the aspects of the Psyche, also noted above, are conscious, subconscious, and superconscious. These modes of mind can be seen like phases and can be compared to water, H_2O, which can be a gas, liquid, or solid. Water can take a different form or state, but it is the same element. Ice and steam seem quite different but have the same chemical composition and represent phase states.

In the analogy of H_2O the light of the Soul is like the vapor state of water and the human body, like ice, is the solid form, moving in and out of incarnation. The Psyche can also be imagined like the electro-magnetic spectrum, which has a range of frequencies, vibration, and amplitude. The spectrum is a continuum that expresses at different wavelengths. Visible light is one portion of the larger spectrum with infrared and ultra violet at either end of that portion. Like the continuum of visible light, certain frequencies may denote what we perceive as the colors red or green, but the shift is gradual along the continuum, and the exact point at which red changes to orange is difficult to discern.

Our Psyche is also a continuum, and as shown by our brain waves, the shift in awareness along the continuum is extreme at the ends—wide awake or asleep—but at any given moment our consciousness may be at different wavelengths. I believe that what we call consciousness is like a sliding scale, and we can train ourselves to modulate our brain waves, and therefore our state of mind, with intention. If we are sleepy we can drop into a deeper state to regenerate. If we are stressed we can meditate to relax, and we can also learn to shift into the high gear of gamma brain waves when we need inspiration.

Using a computer analogy, our Psyche is like a multi-core computer operating in a multi-tasking operating system. Our brain is like the hardware and our consciousness is the software that runs the programs. What is stored in the brain is not the experience, and increasingly research is indicating that memory is not limited to the brain. Like the Cloud and the Internet, we are connected to a large and complex memory network. A permeable barrier exists between self-consciousness and para-consciousness (see page 48), and indeed they may be thought of as "parallel processors."

States of Consciousness

What has been typically called the conscious mind looks outward to the world of form and makes choices. We have been largely conditioned to believe that what we think of as waking consciousness—everyday life—is primary, most important, and captures most of our attention. What is usually called subconscious, or unconscious, is more inner-directed, driving physical as well as psychological homeostasis. The aspect of our nature that we think of as spirit, our Soul, is our true essence and remains in what might be called the world of spirit, containing the memories of all of our lifetimes.

Given this confusing state of linguistic affairs, and after months of reflection, I am proposing new terms for these aspects of our Psyche that might better express the "modes of mind." Rather than the conventional terms of conscious, subconscious, and superconscious, which I argue have inherent but somewhat unfortunate hierarchical implications, my reflection suggests terms that I hope might be more useful.

After a good deal of cognitive work and meditation I offer these alternatives: self-conscious; para-conscious (former subconscious) and meta-conscious (former superconscious). Para is from ancient Greek, meaning "beside" or "side-by-side" and expresses what I have come to better understand as the relationship of this aspect of our Psyche with self-consciousness, our waking awareness. Meta is also from Greek, and means "transcendent" or "beyond," and is what we think of as our Soul or Higher Self.

Self-consciousness – the waking mind

Self-consciousness is the intellect and the ego with a small "e" and is the waking personality, the chooser and decider that looks both outward at the world of physical appearance and inward through thought. This is the personality, the thinker, rational mind, sensing, and temporal orientation. Self-consciousness is the realm of clock time and language. This part of our Psyche identifies with the current lifetime's sense of "self" and personality, navigating the physical world, learning new things, making choices, and getting consequences.

Self-consciousness is moved by a sunrise, feels loss when a loved one dies, aspires to achievement and longs for meaning. Our need for security and affection, and our ambition to achieve are focused through self-consciousness. Self-consciousness is also where our judgments and prejudices reside. This aspect of our Psyche tends to ignore or deny messages from dreams because it is the nature of the waking mind to resist what is unknown or face material that tends to challenge beliefs and opinions.

Like the electro-magnetic spectrum, where visible light is only a small segment, self-consciousness may be like the 5% of reality that can be measured. This is the aspect of our triune nature that we typically most identify with and that occupies most of our attention. Self-consciousness is the lens through which we look outward to the world of the senses and the perception of what seems to be concrete reality. Until we embark on a spiritual quest, and begin to connect with what's normally cloaked from everyday awareness, our minds live mostly in this arena.

The Tibetan Master Djwal Khul, through the writing of Alice Bailey in her book *Estoteric Astrology* said, "Instinct, governing the vegetable and animal kingdoms, develops into intellect in the human family. Later intellect merges into intuition and intuition into illumination. When the superhuman consciousness is evoked these two—intuition and illumination—take the place of instinct and of intelligence." And in the book, *From Intellect to Intuition,* Bailey writes, "Development of the intellect is necessary but as a means to an end and one step on the way to a fully awakened and active mental body." I would say a fully functioning Psyche.

Para-consciousness – the Parallel Processor

Para-consciousness allows for the development of intuition. The para-conscious is automatic and responsive, and until we awaken spiritually, is the part of our Psyche that is more directly connected to the Soul. Para-consciousness beats our hearts, circulates our blood, moves breath through our lungs, and digests our food, bringing the various systems of the body into homeostasis. We chew and swallow our food but don't stop to think about the diverse and complex processes involved in digestion and assimilation. This realm could be analogous to the 27% that is called dark matter and is connected to the "field" of universal consciousness.

Para-consciousness is always on duty whether our self-conscious mind is awake or asleep. Our self-conscious mind becomes dormant while we sleep, while para-consciousness (subconscious) remains fully awake—science has shown that we still hear and process everything even while asleep. Para-consciousness is the reservoir of our feelings that arise from prior experiences. This aspect of our Psyche is timeless and symbolic. Para-consciousness contains what we are unaware of at the self-conscious level, as well as our memories, and has the capacity to link with and draw upon what Jung called the Collective Unconscious, which is a vast reservoir of the memories of the Universe.

Para-consciousness manages long-term memory and mastered skills. In computer terms, para-consciousness is like a simultaneous co-processor. We learned to ride a bicycle and drive a car and we may have memorized the words to a nursery rhyme as a child. We can recite multiplication tables, and some of us can speak more than one language. When we learn to dance or play a sport, a dynamic relationship develops between our self-conscious and para-conscious modes. At the beginning the process is "conscious," counting steps, learning notes, practicing pitches and catches.

Over time, the training is encoded in memory and motions and performance become automatic. We learn to dance and no longer have to count the steps. We reach up to catch a fly ball in center field, or play a sonata from memory. Musicians, dancers, and athletes have learned through intense training to have self-consciousness and para-consciousness work together to express skill and sometimes mastery.

Famed pianist Vladimir Horowitz was reputed to say, "The worst thing that can befall a concert pianist is to think about the position of his fingers."

Seen another way, our Psyche is like a garden. A gardener initially sets the layout of the garden, tills the soil, and chooses what to plant. A gardener also waters, fertilizes, and removes weeds that would otherwise choke the plants. But it is Nature, like our para-conscious mind, that grows the plants. I believe what has been called the subconscious, which I am now calling para-consciousness, or the para-conscious, has been misunderstood. This amazing aspect of our Psyche has often been questionably described as a robotic servant. Given the miraculous functions of para-consciousness, this seems not only inaccurate but demeaning. I now believe the truth is both more subtle and complex.

I believe we are meant to work in a more intentional and respectful way with this aspect of our Psyche to enhance information flow from our Soul, meta-consciousness, that will enhance healing and spiritual growth. I believe self-consciousness needs to recognize para-consciousness as an equal partner, deserving of respect. When these modes of mind operate as a "pair," our capacities are enhanced. We need to honor our inner life as much as our outer world of physical appearances.

Because I now experience the aspect of my Psyche I call para-conscious as a powerful partner, a silent twin, I have given her a name so I could acknowledge all she does and be constantly grateful. I call her Jeanie, which is a play on words of "genie," a magical mythical being like the one who inhabited Aladdin's lamp. Genie comes from the Arabic word *jinni*. What has become key to this relationship is I have learned to ask for her help and to slip into a "listening" mode, like the receive setting on a walkie-talkie.

One amazing experience of working with Jeanie, my para-conscious, was an incident where I was looking for a book. I had repeatedly searched for the book without success, and thought perhaps I had loaned it to a friend. In the manner I've learned, I dropped into a purposeful state and asked for her help. Almost instantly, my eyes were drawn to a spot on a bookshelf where I had already looked several times. To my amazement, there was the book--invisible only moments before.

My self-conscious state was blind to the book, but para-consciousness knew how to find it, even though the book was placed on the shelf by my husband, and I had no awareness of the book's location. This is only one example of how we can profoundly benefit from acknowledging para-conscious, and I am still learning to work with this amazing aspect of my Psyche.

Meta-consciousness – the Soul, our Higher Self

Meta-conscious is the aspect of our Psyche that lives in eternity, the Soul, our Higher Self, projecting or radiating a part of our eternal essence into an incarnation in space-time. Meta, as noted above, is also from Greek and means "transcendent" or "beyond," partaking of cosmic consciousness. This might be analogous to the realm of dark energy—the 68% of reality that exists on the largest of scales. After lifetimes of work and progress, gathering experiences through projected lifetimes in space-time, at some point along the spiritual path, self-consciousness awakens to our true nature and meta-consciousness begins to infuse the personality with greater wisdom.

In esoteric traditions the Soul, meta-consciousness, is considered to be a "spark of the divine," but how does the Soul's energy manifest in space-time? When I reflected on this at different times, one day I received a spontaneous vision in meditation. The idea was so intense and striking that I searched for an image that might portray what I had seen. The artist Luis Calcada's (European Southern Observatory) impression included in the diagram to the right of what I am calling "Anatomy of the Psyche" is of a magnetar, a type of a neutron star with an extremely powerful magnetic field. This is almost exactly how meta-consciousness appears in my meditations.

It is beyond the scope of this book to claim certain knowledge of the nature of the Soul, the wisest part of the Psyche, either philosophically, psychologically, or from the realm of quantum physics. However, we can draw on ancient traditions and modern testimony for language and concepts, and the diagram hopefully offers a visual aid for our intuition.

I have come to perceive the Soul, meta-consciousness, as a luminous sphere made of photons, spinning at the speed of light like a vortex, a toroidal hypersphere. The illustration below is an attempt to depict my vision. This whirling brilliance is the ground of our being and the presence of our existence in eternity. During an incarnation a portion of this radiant essence projects into space-time, expressing through our personalities. Like the phases of H20 analogy, water has memory, and the photons that form the Soul also have memory. In the realm of spirit this sphere is seen as a color of the rainbow as described by Dr. Michael Newton's clients. The Soul, meta-consciousness, becomes a vessel for all it has experienced with an advancement through higher states, higher frequencies, ultimately to a sort of violet iridescence.

Anatomy of the Psyche

Once we recognize the triune nature of our Psyche, as shown in the illustration above, we can open a more constructive communication channel to reestablish mental and emotional equilibrium. We know the physical body works toward homeostasis, which is a balancing of all systems, a tendency toward a relatively stable internal state that persists despite changes in the external world. Through para-consciousness, our Psyche operates not only the physical homeostasis of our bodies but also our psycho-emotional equilibrium.

The Psyche is a system, a unity, that is intended to be balanced, just like in the physical body; it is our para-conscious that is the agent of equilibrium. In addition to all the functions the para-conscious manages through the autonomic system, this part of our Psyche provides feedback to the self-conscious mind when we have made good choices or unfortunate ones.

As we grow spiritually, what has been called "conscience" also grows in strength. This aspect of our nature prompts us to improve and manage our lower urges. Conscience has been defined an inner feeling or voice that acts a guide, showing the rightness or wrongness of behavior. This can manifest as a guilty conscience or having feelings of remorse. Common metaphors for conscience include the "voice within," or the "inner light." Para-consciousness may function as an aspect of conscience, originating at the level of the Soul, through dream messages.

Socrates used the Greek term *"daimonic* sign," in this context, which he described as an inner voice heard when someone was about to make a mistake. To the Greeks a *daimon* (not demon) was a helpful and positive divine being, or supernatural power, like the religious idea of an angel on the shoulder.

Dreams are a primary way that our Psyche brings our mind and emotions into balance and are also the voice of conscience. Para-conscious provides feedback through dreams and synchronicities, but at first, we are usually unaware of their teaching significance. We may believe that our dreams are only random and insignificant, and that synchronicities are mere coincidences. When we begin to acknowledge how the Soul or meta-consciousness speaks through the symbolic language of para-consciousness, the messages become more apparent and understandable.

Para-consciousness manages most ordinary feedback and integration from both the physical and psychological realms, usually without our awareness. However, when feedback has been ignored, and circumstances become more critical, meta-consciousness, our Soul, our fount of higher wisdom, raises the stakes, and physical symptoms and dream symbols become more difficult to ignore. This can bring more vivid and memorable dreams along with synchronicities and serendipities that are orchestrated by the Soul to penetrate our resistance and denial just like the golden scarab story told in Chapter 1.

Although most dream content is relatively standard feedback to maintain equilibrium in the Psyche, just like most adjustments para-conscious makes to keep our physical body healthy, in both cases there are times when an alarm is sounded. Again, in many cases, self-consciousness ignores this feedback until uncertainty and conflict become extreme and can no longer be denied.

In the next chapter we will explore how the Psyche manifests in waking consciousness as we journey through time, and examine what we need to learn about our own reincarnating nature to be able to undertake the passage with deeper understanding and a greater sense of purpose?

Julie Loar

CHAPTER SIX

Out of Darkness: The Soul's Journey

*Armed with the key of charity, of love and tender mercy,
thou art secure before the Gate of Dana,
the gate that stands at the entrance to the Path.*

~ The Book of the Golden Precepts

Now that we have a conceptual understanding of the threefold nature of our Psyche, we can gain a better understanding of what has been called the Soul's Journey. Ancient traditions and modern views have described the Soul and its journey and these descriptions are remarkably consistent. This testimony, while separated in time by thousands of years, agrees that our Soul exists in eternity but projects a portion of its essence into a lifetime—an incarnation—to learn and grow. Our true nature is consciousness, and we are on a journey through space-time while simultaneously existing in another dimension.

The Soul's journey is often called the spiritual path, and it's been said that when you are awake you know there is a path. This idea has been taught in diverse cultures from Hinduism to the indigenous tradition of Hawaiian *Huna*. It is not my intention to reinvent what has been transmitted in wise spiritual traditions for thousands of years, but I believe a summary will prove helpful. In simple terms we can think of the spiritual path as stages of development of increasing wisdom and grace over long ages. Like any journey there are milestones, and these markers have been described by many wisdom traditions. A few will be shared in this chapter.

The means for the Soul's journey is reincarnation where a Soul animates a personality for a lifetime. Soul fragments, projections of the Soul's essence, have numerous and diverse incarnations, which over many lifetimes lead out of ignorance into wisdom and out of darkness into light. Between lifetimes the memories of a single recent incarnation are integrated into the Soul, meta-consciousness, as our Higher Self evolves.

In a way that is still a profound mystery, our Soul holds all the life memories that the reincarnating aspect experiences as we slowly grow in light and love. As our Soul also evolves and grows from those experiences this collective wisdom begins to inform our earthly lives, and gradually the Soul's wisdom expresses through the personality. Slowly, we come to recognize who we are and what our purpose is.

Earlier versions of this perennial story were told through two classic works of literature. *The Divine Comedy*, by Dante Alighieri, is a narrative of the state of souls after death and presents an image of divine justice meted out as due punishment or reward and describes Dante's travels through Hell, Purgatory, and Heaven. Considered by many to be one of the great works of literature, the poem is an allegory that represents the soul's journey toward "God," which begins with a recognition

The Soul as Guide, Showing the Way, by William Blake for *Dante's Divine Comedy*: Purgatorio, Canto IV. (Tate Gallery London used with permission).

and rejection of sin *(Inferno)*, followed by the penitent Christian life *(Purgatorio)*, which is followed by the soul's ascent to God *(Paradiso)*.

The Pilgrim's Progress from This World to That Which Is to Come by John Bunyan is a Christian allegory written in 1678. Pilgrim's Progress is regarded as one of the most significant works of theological fiction in English literature and has been translated into more than 200 languages, never going out of print. The entire book is presented as a dream sequence that is narrated by an omniscient narrator. Similar to Dante's *Divine Comedy,* the allegory's protagonist, Christian, journeys from his hometown, the City of Destruction (this world), to the Celestial City (that which is to come) Heaven. These classical stories have struck deep and lasting chords because the essence resonates with truth.

In Chinese tradition the Tao signifies way, path, road, or sometimes doctrine or principle. Spiritually, Tao is seen as the natural order of the universe that human intuition must discern in order to realize the potential of individual wisdom. From the Chinese perspective of Tao, this intuitive knowing cannot be grasped as a concept but can only be learned through the journey of everyday life.

In Hindu tradition the Soul, *Atman* in Sanskrit, is seen to be on a journey through cosmic time--an evolutionary journey back to unity. This journey ultimately leads beyond identification with external phenomena, having experiences that lead to the transcendent self, *Brahman*.

The Mystery Rites of Demeter were celebrated in Greece at Eleusis, which is about fourteen miles from Athens, by participants from all over the known world from 1,600 BCE to 392 CE. The specific details of these secret rituals have never been revealed as the penalty was death. The Mysteries were based on the myth of Demeter and her daughter Persephone, who made an annual descent to Hades, the underworld, and ascended again in spring to enliven the Earth. The myth of Demeter was well known, so scholars have deduced that the rites expressed the return of life as shown through the cycle of the agricultural year. The inherent message was if the fields and flowers are renewed every year why give humans only one brief lifetime. Initiates were apparently given such a powerful vision of cyclical lifetimes through reincarnation that those who participated claimed to no longer fear death and were inspired to live a more noble life.

In a similar vein, and at the same time period in history, the Mysteries of Osiris were celebrated in an annual new year festival at summer solstice in Abydos in Egypt. Osiris was a vegetation god and lord of the Underworld and afterlife whose story also represented overcoming death. These rites also celebrated cyclical renewal and the annual symbolic resurrection of the god Osiris who renewed the great land of Egypt that bordered the Nile river. The rites included a dramatic reenacting of his death, and the magical mating with the goddess Isis, queen of magic, which produced the divine son Horus. The symbolic resurrection of Osiris promised new life and ensured the cyclical rebirth of the land.

Moving forward in time, the Twelve Labors of Hercules, which in Greek myth described the hero, who journeys through twelve labors to atone for his sins, is another version of this timeless tale. This myth has also been interpreted as the symbolic annual journey of the Sun, representing the Soul, as the spiritual aspirant travels through many lifetimes around the wheel of twelve zodiac signs.

The universal idea of the heroic quest was made famous by scholar Joseph Campbell and is another timeless version of the Soul's story. The hero, who is each of us, receives a call and departs on a quest. There are stages of the quest, and Campbell's research found this mythic pattern appeared in every culture. Campbell referred to this as a "monomyth," which he perceived to be like an archetypal expression. Simplified these stages are call, departure, descent, and return. If successful, the transformed hero (or heroine) becomes deified with gifts that are meant to be shared with others in service.

Modern Testimony

The trance readings of Virginia Beach psychic Edgar Cayce shared the previous lives/incarnations and current lessons of thousands of individuals who came to him for "life readings." Choices, patterns, and relationships were revealed, offering insight and guidance to those who received these trance sessions. In his wonderful book, *Bowl of Light*, shamanic teacher Hank Wesselman, PhD, shared the powerful teachings told to Wesselman by Kahuna elder Hale Makua, his long-time friend in Hawaii. Wesselman shared Makua's description of the idea of the Soul's journey from the indigenous teachings of Hawaii that according to the elder are at least 12,000 years old.

Huna, or more accurately, *Ho'omana*, means "hidden" and this knowledge was kept secret in an oral tradition for thousands of years. Hale Makua gifted Wesselman with these teachings, as much as he felt appropriate, and Wesselman has shared them with the world. Makua taught that the Huna word, and idea of *Aumakua*, meant "immortal soul." He said Makua means "parent" and *au* means "time." So, the personal Aumakua is our parent in time, our Higher Self, our Soul. Makua said,

> This includes all your ancestors, who were your past selves, and who are archived within the energetic field of your Higher Self (Soul). Through the so-called subconscious aspect we are in constant connection to our Aumakua, our higher mind of light, that communicates directly with us during life through the medium of intuition and inspiration—through insight and through dreams and visions.

The pioneering work of psychotherapist and author Michael Newton, PhD, who worked with thousands of clients in hypnosis over his long career, provides a framework in the language and experience of contemporary people. Dr. Newton's clients came from diverse walks of life and different religious and philosophical belief systems, but over the course of many decades their trance sessions revealed different levels of Soul development. These individuals presented a stunning consistency of testimony about the purpose and plan of earthly life, the between lives state, and the nature of the Soul's journey.

Newton's outstanding books, *Journey of Souls* and *Destiny of Souls*, describe the process of Soul growth and earthly life experiences in great detail through client sessions. A complex and compelling picture emerges from people from our time that perfectly aligns with ancient wisdom teachings. Dr. Newton's legacy includes the institute he founded for this work and the training of other therapists to continue his legacy. *https://www.newtoninstitute.org*

Like ancient wisdom traditions, Newtons clients described a process whereby the Soul, whose main essence always remains in the "spirit world," projects a portion of itself into physical incarnation for the purpose of gathering experience, learning lessons, and facing tests that will ultimately, and over time, promote spiritual growth. In between lives, the Soul fragment returns to the Soul's essence and the developing Soul spends time evaluating choices, progress, and results that were achieved in the lifetime.

Life in form is a school, and the Soul slowly grows in wisdom and understanding through this process. The Soul fragment in earthly life may have made progress, or taken a few steps backward, and needs to plan a course correction in the next incarnation. The between lives period is a busy time of healing, evaluating, and planning for the next sojourn into the world of form.

In addition, Newton's clients said that each Soul has a Spirit Guide, an advanced being who remains with the evolving Soul throughout all the incarnations from "birth" as a new Soul until "graduation" when the growing and evolving being has learned enough to become a Guide. Our Spirit Guides, like guardian angels, remain with us through the long journey from innocence to enlightenment. This idea aligns with what is taught in Theosophy, and the books of Alice A. Bailey, about the Solar Angel, a being of great love and wisdom who watches over our reincarnating aspect like a guardian, or a mother with a child, through the ages long journey.

Dr. Newton's clients, and other teachers from ancient traditions, have described an ongoing process where Souls move through a long evolutionary path. For a very long time our incarnating aspect is unaware of this long journey and the connection and relationship with the Soul. Newton's clients also consistently described a council of very advanced beings who help evaluate our progress. This was not described as judge and jury but rather as wise and compassionate input from a very high level of spiritual awareness.

Parallel to what other ancient traditions have taught, Newton's clients described the advancement of the Soul as expressing through a series of seven stages expressed as colors from white in the youngest souls to lavender purple in those who were ready to "graduate" and go on to being guides themselves. We can take heart that there is a template, a blueprint of becoming, but unlike our biological development, which happens automatically, our spiritual development requires our conscious and willing participation. At some point we must take ourselves in hand and do the work required to grow spiritually.

According to Newton's thousands of clients, we also belong to a soul group of about ten other Souls, who are at our same relative level of development, and with whom we repeatedly reconnect in earthly lives and in between. Newton's clients described how in between lives we share successes and perceived failures, get feedback, evaluate our progress, and plan for the next lifetime. Consistent reports from Newton's clients relate that during our lifetimes we cast other members from our soul group as characters in our life dramas, and we return again and again to help each other grow.

We are drawn to members of our soul group through prior agreement to work on our issues and challenges. Sometimes our most difficult tests come from those with whom we have the deepest bonds. This is vital to remember as we face challenges from some of the people in our lives. Newton's clients also consistently reported that we also have numerous experiences on other worlds and in other star systems.

✻　✻　✻

Our eternal Soul is on a journey through space-time, through many diverse incarnations, on its way to enlightenment. These experiences are diverse, ranging from queens to servants, warriors to healers, each offering lessons, gifts, and tests. We go from monarch to peasant, depending on what must be learned or resolved. And we are part of a greater interconnected wholeness. The Soul integrates many lifetimes through a great variety of incarnational experiences in different personalities, genders, and social circumstances based on the karma generated and the lessons desired.

The reincarnating aspect of our Psyche is like an actor in a play or movie who acts out a different character in every production, but is always the same person behind the role. In a similar way, the Soul projects its essence into an incarnation, which is like a temporary acting role, but at the end of a lifetime that experience becomes part of the collective of the eternal Soul. In another analogy, we might think of incarnations like trips we take in this lifetime. A vacation takes us out of our normal experience, and when we return, we integrate the trip into our life experience. One trip to a foreign country doesn't define a lifetime, but what's learned can inform future decisions.

Early in our Soul's journey we are unaware of our purpose and we move through many lifetimes, making choices and getting consequences, without making much forward progress. This story was brilliantly told in the 1993 movie Groundhog Day where actor Bill Murray's character Phil Connors becomes trapped in a time loop that forces him to repeat Groundhog Day, the second day of February. Each morning he wakes to an exact repeat of the day before, spending nearly a decade until he begins to see how his own behavior and choices are keeping him stuck in a vicious cycle.

Like Murray's character Phil, at some point we too begin to recognize our patterns, eventually becoming more aware and striving to undertake the journey more consciously. At this stage we begin to connect with our Soul, our Higher Self who lives in eternity, and the light of our Soul slowly dawns in the mind of our personality.

Our Soul watches and waits through long ages until our reincarnating self/ego awakens, and learns to hear our Soul's voice, offering guidance. Then the "child" connects with the "parent" and a transformation begins. The orientation of earthly life shifts perspective and takes on greater spiritual purpose. Increasingly life takes on greater meaning, and spiritual progress and growth are quickened, as the ego/personality becomes what has been called "Soul-infused," and the stages of the Path are more illumined.

But what is the nature of this Path, and once this journey beckons, how do we respond?

Julie Loar

CHAPTER SEVEN

The Path of Holiness: The Map

Thou canst not travel on the Path
before thou hast become the Path itself.

~ The Voice of the Silence, Chosen Fragments from the Book of the Golden Precepts,
translated and annotated by Helena P. Blavatsky

So far, we have explored the nature of our brain, our esoteric anatomy, and our consciousness, the Psyche. We know that our process of growth takes place over many lifetimes. What can we learn about the long journey and how we can frame our progress in a single lifetime?

The perceived truth of our Soul's perennial journey has resonated through time. Ancient wisdom traditions affirm that many lifetimes are required to learn the necessary lessons and grow into our potential. Although the realm of the Soul is light and love, on our journey through space-time, we can through ignorance choose darkness and fear as we stumble, sometimes failing to learn our lessons. Our awakening to our destiny may come suddenly through a profound life experience, or we may slowly emerge from the dark cave of our ignorance and move into the steadily increasing light of becoming. Either way the great plan of the Cosmos leads always toward union.

Waking life is like a lucid dream, and we are the dreamer, sleeping until we awaken and remember our purpose. As we choose, and receive the consequences of our choices, slowly we learn. At some critical point in our long journey a spark of divine fire from the Soul, meta-consciousness, ignites the flame of aspiration in our hearts.

This flame grows into a radiance as we walk the path of the sacred and do the work required. Our heart begins to beat with compassion in a rhythm that connects us to others and the Universe.

Eastern traditions, where this knowledge has survived, and in the Hermetic tradition, where the teachings went underground, both tell the same tale. The stages of the journey have been described as the Way of Discipleship and the Path of Initiation in both Eastern and Western traditions as well as in a similar manner in the teachings of Theosophy and the Hawaiian tradition of Huna. Ancient wisdom has been guarded in secret in the high mountains of Earth from the Andes to Hawaii and the Himalayas. Increasingly, the wisdom keepers are sharing their knowledge since the planet is in peril. We are called to awaken.

Earth is a school and our gradual spiritual awakening happens as we pass through Twelve Gates of Discipleship and Five Initiations. This process can be slow, working with the long cycles of the ages, or hastened, "quickened," which results in a more rapid unfoldment of the power and life of meta-conscious.

Discipleship

The Path of Discipleship is the stage of evolution where one becomes self-aware and willingly submits to a "forcing" process where the will of the Soul, meta-consciousness, is imposed upon the lower nature-ego and personality. This is so the flower of the Soul can unfold its petals more quickly. This involves an acceleration of karma that has to be discharged, and from the standpoint of earthly life, brings what appears to be suffering and loss but also continuing revelation and a greater sense of purpose.

In *The Bowl of Light* by Hank Wesselman, PhD, Hawaiian elder Hale Makua summarizes aspects of initiation, saying "To get to knowledge you have to know who you are, and you have to eliminate your fears. And when you achieve knowledge, you must maintain silence, so you don't deprive others of the power that comes with their own discoveries."

That sounds remarkably like the ancient wisdom of the Sphinx—to know, to will, to dare, and to keep silent.

In *First Principles of Theosophy*, in a chapter titled The Path of Discipleship, author C. Jinarajadasa, MA, describes the stages of discipleship, ending with initiation as:

Person of ideals

Probationary pupil

Accepted pupil

Child of the Master

Initiate

While we move through the stages of discipleship we are said to be on the wheel with twelve spokes, the Wheel of the Zodiac signs, which are twelve gates of life experience. Sometimes these stages are described as The Living Way, twelve symbolic Gates of the Sun, or gates of light. These gates allow for lifetimes on the wheel of time that present our life lessons, our tests and trials. "The *Way*, which leads to the Heart of God, sweeps in a circle through twelve great Gates. Cycle after cycle the Gates open and the Gates close. The human children of God, march along in these cycles. Slowly we pass through the pillars between the Gates and learn our lessons in the Halls of Discipline." (Alice A. Bailey, *The Labors of Hercules*).

Lifetimes of lessons, passing through the twelve sign portals, prepare the aspirant for the five stages of Initiation that follow. The myth of the Twelve Labors of Hercules encodes this knowledge where the karmic labors of atonement of the hero align with the twelve signs. Like the mythical hero Hercules, who symbolizes the traveler on this journey, the Sun symbolizes the Soul in esoteric astrology.

In *A Treatise on White Magic*, Alice A. Bailey says, "What is a disciple? He or she is one who seeks to learn a new rhythm, to enter a new field of experience, and to follow the steps of advanced humanity who have trodden the path ahead, leading from darkness to light, from the unreal to the real."

The pattern of seven appears in diverse systems, including alchemy, the seven chakras, the notes of the scale, days of the week, and the lunar cycle, which is four phases of seven days. The symbolism of Tarot includes seven stages of spiritual unfoldment, or spiritual activations, that are described in the last seven keys of the Major Arcana. In the symbolic Fool's Journey of Tarot, these can be viewed as the ascent from the valley where the Fool first descended to begin his journey to the final ascent where the Hermit holds his lantern aloft on the high mountain that represents spiritual attainment.

Stages of Illumination in Tarot

Darkness	15	Devil
Lightning	16	Tower
Star light	17	Star
Moon light	18	Moon
Sun light	19	Sun
Astral light	20	Judgment
Cosmic consciousness	21	World

The darkness represented in Tarot by the Devil is the first stage of our spiritual development where we become consciously aware that we in a state of bondage, stuck in a state of pure survival. This awareness is followed by an awakening such as a Near Death Experience. This trigger brings about the third stage, which is an ardent search for truth and desire for a deeper meaning in life.

As more knowledge is attained in the fourth stage the disciple faces character flaws, purging and clearing karma in a more intense manner. As this process unfolds our heart opens, and at the fifth stage we are able to radiate love and goodwill. At the sixth stage the sense of separateness dissolves and there is a growing sense of unity with all things. At the final seventh stage the veil between the worlds disappears and we are ready for conscious service and prepared to step on the Path of Initiation.

This knowledge, and the pattern of seven, is echoed in the Roman Catholic tradition where seven sacraments are viewed as initiations: baptism, confirmation, eucharist, penance, anointing the sick, marriage, and holy orders. The sacraments are seen as mystical channels of divine grace that were instituted by Jesus. The sacraments are divided into three categories: sacraments of initiation, sacraments of healing, and sacraments of service. Each is celebrated with a visible rite, which reflects the invisible spiritual essence of the sacrament.

Reprising seven stages, in Dr. Michael Newton's work, described in Chapter 6, a progression of Soul growth, or evolution, is demonstrated through what his clients described as a "color spectrum of soul auras." (*Destiny of Souls,* page 171). Dr. Newton reported in his second book that he was unaware of this progression when he wrote his first book, *Journey of Souls.* In hindsight he realized that as a therapist he was working with young souls in crisis. With the success of the first book he was contacted by a wider range of soul development from across the country. Based on the subsequent trance testimony of numerous and diverse different clients, who had a range of soul development, Newton proposed seven grades of soul development that were expressed as rainbow colors. His clients described them as:

1. White — Beginning soul
2. Red — Advancing soul
3. Yellow — Teacher
4. Green — Healer
5. Blue — Master
6. Blue-violet — Ascended Master
7. Purple/violet — Higher levels approaching "divinity."

While working on this book I had a number of powerful dreams, several of which will be recounted and interpreted later in Chapter 13. One powerful and transforming dream had a central symbol of "seven stone steps," which revealed and coalesced a critical way to work with dreams. I was profoundly impacted by this dream and the power of the seven stone steps. That revelation led to what is, for me, the main practical message of this book.

Initiation

When we are ready to advance from the level of striving disciples, we arrive at the point of the first of five initiations. We move off the cyclic wheel of rebirth, symbolized by the Zodiac, and step onto the Path proper, sometimes called the Path of Holiness, or the Path of Illumination. Ghandi has said, "The Path is the goal," and other teachers have remarked that when you know there is a Path, you are awake.

After the stages of discipleship, we are prepared to step on the Path proper. In the book, *Masters & the Path*, C.W. Leadbeater describes four qualifications that must be attained during the period of Discipleship before entering the Path of Initiation:

1. Discrimination
2. Desirelessness (do the thing for the sake of rightness; integrity)
3. Six points of good conduct
   Quietude
   Subjugation (mastery of words and actions)
   Cessation of bigotry (wide and generous tolerance)
   Endurance/forbearance – acceptance of karma
   Intention – one-pointedness
   Faith – trust in self and process
4 Longing for liberation

In her book, *Initiation, Human & Solar*, Alice A. Bailey says,

> Initiation leads to the cave within whose circumscribing walls the pairs of opposites are known, and the secret of good and evil is revealed. This leads to the Cross and to that utter sacrifice that must transpire before perfect liberation can be attained, and the initiate stands free of all earth's fetters, held by naught in the three worlds. The Path leads through the Hall of Wisdom, and puts into one's hands the key to all information, systemic and cosmic, in graduated sequence.

This reveals the hidden mystery that lies at the heart of the solar system and leads from one state of consciousness to another. As each state is entered the horizon enlarges, the vista extends, and the comprehension includes more and more, until the expansion reaches a point where the self can embrace all selves, including all that is 'moving and unmoving,' as phrased by an ancient Scripture.

Initiation is a process that quickens evolution and is a gradual expansion of consciousness. The Path of Initiation is considered to be a choice, and not an automatic process, but once chosen accelerates the process of spiritual unfoldment and further intensifies karma in order to balance the scales and clear the debt. The first two initiations are now considered to be preparatory, learning to control the physical and emotional vehicles. The Soul, our meta-consciousness that lies beyond ordinary awareness, can only directly express through physical vehicles and emotional natures that have become steady and balanced. The third initiation is said to achieve control of the mental body. Aart Jurriaanse, South African author and esoteric scholar, has written,

> To the Spiritual Hierarchy the first two initiations recognized by esotericists in describing human spiritual development are preliminary or preparatory stages. What is known as the Third Initiation they regard as the First Major Initiation because at this stage the disciple really becomes 'transfigured' and consciously enters the spiritual kingdom. This marks the stage when the Soul gains control over the mental vehicle, which together with the physical and emotional bodies, constitutes the 'personality.' For the first time the Soul is in full control of the personality. Personality and Soul become fused into a single unit, what has been called a Soul-infused being. This is the consummation of a life, and for the Soul means liberation.

The life of the probationer and disciple prepares the individual for the Path of Initiation. It marks that phase of spiritual unfoldment when the person deliberately and consciously begins to co-operate with the evolutionary forces and works at the reconstruction and strengthening of character. The individual becomes aware of certain shortcomings and systematically tries to rectify what is lacking, to cultivate better qualities and bring the coordinated personality under control of the Soul.

At this point we become more aware of our true nature and the Soul's "voice" and guidance becomes more strongly felt. *In First Principles of Theosophy,* C. Jinarajadasa, MA, says "over time the personality becomes steadily more a reflex of the Higher Ego, which begins to draw on powers of the Monad. The Soul is in truth the highest part of us, which is the Monad." At this stage self-consciousness begins to consciously connect to eternity and our Higher Self, and our meta-consciousness is able to express through self-consciousness. When this happens, the Soul can more directly influence our waking awareness. At this level of awareness, the communication between para-consciousness and self-consciousness is also much more fluid and life is characterized by what might earlier have been imagined as miracles. I offer this modified version of the Anatomy of the Psyche as a way to visualize the awakened connection.

Soul-Infused Personality

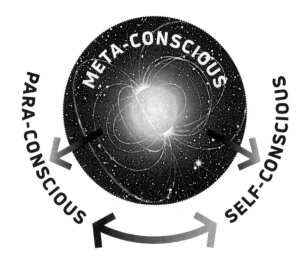

In the Buddhist tradition these stages of Initiation on the Path of Holiness are described as four stages of purification before enlightenment. At the first Initiation the disciple is said to "enter the stream."

Sotapanna	Entering the stream	Accumulation of wisdom and virtue
Sakadagami	Once-returning	Added effort and intensified practice
Anagami	Not returning	Initial enlightenment
Arahat	Venerable	True cultivation of practice
Aseka	Master	No more learning

Buddhist initiation rituals can occur in a public ceremony where a lay follower of Buddhism receives certain Buddhist precepts. Ceremonies differ widely by country and by school of Buddhism. In South Korea the ritual, called *sugye* in Sanskrit, involves formally taking refuge in the Three Jewels of Buddhism: the Buddha, the Dharma, and the Sangha. The initiate also accepts the five precepts: do not kill, do not steal, misuse of sense, wrong speech, and use of intoxicants. During the *sugye* ritual, an initiate is touched with a burning incense stick that leaves a permanent mark, reminding the initiate of the promise to uphold the five precepts. During (or right after) the ceremony the initiate is given a Buddhist name.

In the books by Alice Bailey in the Theosophical tradition the five initiations are connected to five of the chakras, the energy centers in the body, and are also described after critical events in the life of Jesus, some of which became Christian sacraments:

Heart	Birth to spiritual life—control of physical body
Throat	Baptism—astral/emotional control
Brow	Transfiguration—mental control; clairvoyance and clairaudience "eye of mind" telepathy (light from above)
Crucifixion	Perfected human *Arhat* (Pali) *Paramahamsa* (Sanskrit) minor siddhis
Resurrection	Spiritual mastery

Ancient wisdom teaches that some who have graduated and advanced beyond us can choose to remain as guides and teachers, and although they are generally veiled from our eyes, they stand ready to assist. These teachers have been called by many names: The Council of Light, Masters of the Hidden Brotherhood, Mahatmas, and Brotherhood of Light. These wise and compassionate beings are in service to the spiritual hierarchy and spiritual aspirants.

Modern Relevance—Rites of Passage

In Theosophical literature the rites of Initiation happen with great import and ceremony in out-of-the-body experiences. Perhaps in the ancient temples of Atlantis and Egypt these rites occurred in the physical body. In our modern world a veil conceals the reality of these powerful ancient traditions and ceremonies. How do we find relevance in our busy modern world? Even though this knowledge is hidden or "occulted," the pattern of our spiritual unfoldment is still present in our DNA.

Initiations in the modern world may come in the form of what we often call "rites of passage" such as a life-threatening illness, a near-death experience, loss, trauma, or the death of a loved one. These experiences can change us at depth and reorient our lives. Life-altering occurrences have the capacity to transform us. While we deal with grief and loss we are usually unaware of our transformation, until in hindsight, we realize how our hearts have become more compassionate and we are more likely to share the pain and grief of others.

I found a quote on the site www.StreetPoets.com that said, "When we see life through an initiatory lens, death becomes an ally, or guide. Through initiation, radical growth becomes possible."

When we live with the knowledge that there is a Path, our lives have a greater sense of purpose and meaning, and we are ready to work with our dreams in earnest and to learn the language of the Soul.

Part Two

Dreamwork Fundamentals

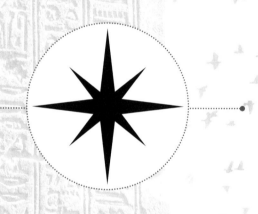

From the unreal lead me to the Real,
from darkness lead me to Light,
from death lead me to immortality.

~ Alcyone, *At the Feet of the Master*

CHAPTER EIGHT

Dreamwork Fundamentals:
Types of Dreams & Eight Common Dream Motifs

Dreams are letters the Self (Soul) writes to us every night.

~ Marie-Louise von Franz, PhD, *The Way of the Dream*

In Part Two we'll cover basic principles of dream work and dive deep into the serious and fulfilling aspect of the work. We will explore the nature of symbols and other types of dreams and dreamlike experiences. I will discuss synchronicities and the idea of serendipity as well offer a *Seven-Step* process for working with dreams that came as a result of a profound dream. I will also interpret several dreams I had while writing this book that have acted as coaches, counselors, and cheerleaders.

Even if we take good care and have good habits, sometimes we can become ill. There is also a spectrum of mental health, which can relate to trauma and stress, and the dreams of a spiritual aspirant will likely be different in content and meaning from someone suffering from mental or physical illness or severe depression. My strong advice is that readers of this book will seek professional guidance if you are in crisis. Sometimes we need other kinds of support.

Research in sleep clinics increasingly demonstrates the critical nature of sleep and dreams in memory and overall physical and mental health, and studies show that we all dream every night for two hours, regardless of what we remember. Therefore, given the number of dreams we have in a month, potentially sixty hours, it's apparent that most do not merit deep study and intense analysis. We learned in Chapter 3 that we go through four to six sleep cycles per night. Let's say for argument's sake that we dream in each of those cycles—that's an average of five dreams each night. Five dreams a night, multiplied by thirty days in an average month, is a possible 150 dreams each month and 1800 dreams in a year. Even if we remembered all those dreams, spending hours a day interpreting them would not be productive. I believe para-consciousness prioritizes the messages, and we remember dreams that deserve attention.

From the expanding viewpoint of scientific research, the vast majority of dreams serve as routine processing and filing of life events, shifting recall from short term memory into the mysterious storehouse of long-term memory. This seems to act as a kind of sorting mechanism to transfer information from the data buffers of short-term memory into storage in the vast warehouse of para-consciousness and what might be the realm of Sheldrake's morphic resonance.

There seems to be a spectrum of dreams that might be described as that of minor messages on one end and main event dreams on the other. Synchronicities and serendipities, because they are rare, fall into the main event category. Walking the Path of expanding consciousness is our goal. We are a work in progress—human "becomings" rather than just human beings. Whether or not we sense where we are on this journey of becoming, we can deepen our passage by working with our dreams. Dreams are like a mirror, a "looking glass," holding up an honest reflection of guidance in symbolic language.

With few exceptions, such as prophetic or lucid dreams that will be described in Chapter 10, most dreams fall into the category of 95-98% that we do not remember. The goal of dream work is to remember the dreams that are significant and instructive and learn to decode and interpret the symbolic language. Jung said "Dream symbols are messengers so the poverty of consciousness can once again remember the forgotten language of symbols." (*Man and His Symbols.*)

Based on my own experience and that of many others I've worked with, the average number of dreams that are sufficiently remembered is about one or two a month. That should be manageable for most of us. Some people do dream more and need to decide how to prioritize their dreams, while other people claim not to recall any dreams. I believe once we ask to remember significant dreams, we will. Even if you remember more, you can choose which dreams seem to have the biggest impact—strong feeling(s) upon waking, or a compelling central symbol. Focus on those.

Most remembered dreams support our personal growth. The testimony of ages is that our dreams can offer counsel in the various aspects of life, bringing the Psyche into equilibrium, and guiding our spiritual path. Para-consciousness holds up a mirror, inviting us to take an honest look at objective feedback. Sometimes we need to make a course correction where we have fallen short, or improve performance in some area or take action to correct an error in judgment. At other times aspects of our growth require encouragement and inspiration to heal self-doubt, or offer hope and confidence where we doubt our talents and abilities. On rare occasions we receive what are often called "big dreams," which are believed to be direct messages from our Higher Self, and from all reports, are received as blessings that remain with us our whole life.

Dream Categories

My own experience, and work with other dreamers, suggests that dreams can be broadly categorized in three ways:

> Feedback about our choices
> Encouragement when we doubt
> Spiritual guidance—Big Dreams

To be frank, most dreams fall into the first category and para-consciousness mirrors back guidance about our "performance." However, some of my most important dreams have come in the form of encouragement when I doubted myself. Big dreams are rare, usually a few in a lifetime, but it's a thrill when one appears.

In any of the three main dream categories the most important thing to notice as you wake is your emotional or mental state. On the one hand you might wake with a strong feeling that lingers from the dream. Dream feelings, what you're experiencing in the dream, seem to foreshadow how things may work out in waking life and are the main clues to the tone of the dream's message. For example if you're feeling fear in a dream, or when you wake, chances are if you recognize and face what frightens you, the issue you're concerned about won't happen.

On the other hand, if your dream is filled with joy, you can expect smooth sailing with the project or person. If anger is present when you wake, look out, as that suppressed emotion may erupt unexpectedly as an emotional storm in waking life. If you are more of a thinking person, then your first thought about the dream and its main symbol may be what stands out. What is uppermost in your awareness as you waken from a remembered dream is what should be noted and journaled.

Feedback Dreams

Feedback dreams may also offer information about deep patterns we're trying to heal through symbols and themes that repeat. Over time, you might see a pattern in how issues relate to one another and determine if a particularly vivid and emotional dream is related to the same issue you have ignored in your waking life, raising the stakes. This feedback affects how we will respond the next time a similar situation appears. These dreams serve to process current events and responses in waking life, although it could be argued that the times we live in seem to make everyday life more intense. Feedback dreams offer a report card from para-consciousness, determining where we did well, or where we need to improve. If we are both wise and brave, we will look into this mirror with fierce honesty.

Physical dreams can be a subset of Feedback Dreams and often address health issues or physical imbalances that reveal themselves through dream symbols. Health or medical dreams can function as early warning signs if recognized for what they are. Death dreams sometimes appear as strong health warnings that are intended to "shock" us. We may need to improve our diet, or pay attention to a low-grade nagging pain, or quit a destructive habit. Nightmares, which are discussed in Chapter 10, can be in this category and be a dramatic attempt to get through to the self-conscious level after repeated attempts at symbolism has been ignored.

Encouragement Dreams

This category of dreams conveys a sense of encouragement and inspiration. They seem to say, "You can do this." The dream I titled *Elephant Takes a Leap* was a powerful dream in the encouragement category. That dream is interpreted in detail in Chapter 13. I was in the early stages of writing this book and having very serious doubts about my ability to do the developing subject justice. In the dream a huge golden elephant leaped across a crevasse—a seemingly impossible task. I woke with a sense that I just had to keep working and writing. The dream counseled that I could make it no matter how unlikely that seemed in the moment. If you are reading these words, I made it!

If we are working to deconstruct a deep and long-term pattern of self-doubt or lack of confidence, we may receive recurring dreams that offer this kind of empowering message. This type of dream often provides ongoing dreams that act like a coaches or sponsors, cheering us along the path. Encouragement dreams are usually accompanied by a sense of happiness, joy, and optimism upon waking.

Big Dreams

The big dream, a "main event" dream, deals with spiritual guidance and contact with our Higher Self and has the purpose of gaining knowledge and power. Spiritual dreams are powerful messages from our Soul or meta-consciousness to self-consciousness. These dreams are remembered for all of our lives and still retain a vivid and "numinous" quality. As we do more work, the nature of our dreams seems to become more spiritual. A dreamer in ancient times who sought guidance at a dream oracle temple at one of the pilgrimage sites, did so in the hope of having a big dream or having one interpreted.

Big dreams usually occur at pivotal stages or significant junctures in our lives and often repeat the same theme in a slightly different way over several nights. Sometimes archetypal material, like a wizard, warrior, healer, or a zodiac figure appear as symbols. Memories of a big dream are vivid and emotion-packed. A big dream can be so dramatic and startling that the experience is like being awake, and the memory remains clear and stark—and does not fade with time. Big dreams have great power, and their messages should be taken seriously.

Eight Common Dream Motifs

Those who have worked extensively with dreams, as well as evidence from my own research and counseling practice, indicates there are eight common dream themes that seem to recur with regularity. This commonality of themes may speak to the intrinsic similarity of the human experience as well as the issues we all deal with. Even though most people don't recall the majority of their dreams, everyone seems to have a familiar repeating pattern that falls into one of the following categories. Although it's a generalization, I believe these common motifs usually appear in dreams that offer feedback where we need to make a change.

Of course this doesn't cover every dream experience, but instead shows a pattern that has significance and may shed light and provide clues to the area of the Psyche that needs to be brought into equilibrium. C. G. Jung's patients often dreamed of becoming very large or very small, like *Alice in Wonderland*.

Flying and falling rank among the top dream themes. Flying, with a thrilling sense of abandon and freedom, may showcase our expanded abilities while in the dream state. These dreams have a sense of power and liberation that is exhilarating, saying we are more than our bodies and physical selves. These dreams give us a glimpse of capacities that are beyond our physical abilities and seem to generate a sense of heightened confidence. Flying dreams can suggest we will soar above our obstacles and challenges.

By contrast, falling seems to be a way of communicating to self-consciousness that we are making a rapid reentry into our physical body and ordinary awareness. Symbolically falling can also be the opposite of flying, telling us that we feel out of control in our waking life, feeling ready to crash and burn. We might feel in a state of freefall in waking life and need a symbolic parachute. How can we slow things down and gain more control?

Feeling unprepared is a common theme and includes performances we need to give for which we are not adequately rehearsed; or hurrying to catch a plane, train, bus or boat. This motif often includes being lost in an airport or a railway station. Losing or misplacing something valuable, especially keys, wallet, purse, or briefcase, is also common. People often dream of searching for their "vehicle" with a sense of urgency, needing to arrive somewhere. Sometimes these dreams include arriving late for an event or appointment. Jung's patients, who were of course in psychiatric treatment, frequently dreamed of fighting with weapons that were useless. These dreams act as warnings and usually reveal very real concerns about where you need to be prepared for something important in waking life.

Attending school dreams are common and may reveal lessons that you are working on in waking life and be related to the larger theme of feeling unprepared. If you dream of attending school, you may be taking steps to get prepared in waking life, or need to. The setting of the school or learning situation might be a classroom or large conference center. This motif might include failing an exam.

Sometimes, this version of "night school" reveals other work or learning our mind is involved in while the body rests and recharges. This could also indicate where specific preparation or training is needed for what is facing you in waking life and be a signal that you need more study. If going to school or preparing for an exam is a frequent dream setting, you might ask what it is you need to learn most.

Climbing a hill, stairs, or mountain may represent an obstacle you are trying to overcome in waking life or challenging work that requires a lot of sustained effort. These dreams can describe a work in progress in waking life and when analyzed, can indicate the level of difficulty you feel as well as what stage in the symbolic ascent you are. What are the conditions in the dream—clear or stormy? Are you near the top or just starting the climb? Do you feel unable to finish, or are you progressing with confidence? Dreaming that you have reached the summit and are feeling satisfied would be an encouragement dream.

Vulnerability is a common dream theme and is often symbolized by being naked or improperly or inadequately dressed in public, or being lost in a crowd. Dreams of frightening animals or being chased, can also appear in this category but may also show up in a nightmare. These dreams can show where you indeed feel vulnerable in relationships or waking challenges you need to face. This sense of vulnerability can show what you are running from or avoiding. Is the threat real, or something you are blowing out of proportion?

Weather and storms are frequent dream settings. Storms almost always suggest emotional issues that aren't being addressed at the self-conscious level, and these storms are preparing to unleash their emotional force in a potentially damaging way in outer life if warnings continue to be ignored. Note the type of storm and if it is approaching or venting its full fury in the moment. Is the threat a looming crisis to be dealt with or able to be avoided upon notification? Are you moving into a storm or seeing clearing skies on the horizon? Clear weather and sunshine can indicate clarity, indicating clear skies ahead.

Teeth falling out is another frequent theme and may suggest that you are feeling guilty about a "biting" comment you might have made to someone the day before. This symbol almost always has something to communicate about careful speech and judgment. Teeth dreams can also suggest that you have bitten off more than you can chew, as the saying goes, and need to evaluate your resources. Should you "spit it out" or "swallow" it? Teeth affect not only physical appearance and sense of self-confidence but also the ability to feed ourselves and be nourished.

Phone call – trying to answer a phone call or make one – is a frequent dream symbol. Today trying to send a text or email is in the same category and may suggest issues of incomplete communication in waking life. This motif often includes repeated unsuccessful efforts to send the communication. Communication dreams can show where you need to listen to someone or speak your truth, honestly expressing what's on your mind instead of remaining silent. You may be receiving a direct communication from para-consciousness in the form of a phone call or text that you need to pay attention to, or are being counseled to gather courage to address a difficult communication that you have been avoiding. Direct forms of communication do come in dreams as we hear people speak to us, see a sign, or read a letter. Sometimes numbers are connected with these dream images. Numbers, which will be covered in Chapter 16, often appear in communication dreams and play the role of timing and dates that need to be considered.

Reflecting on these commonly appearing dream themes may provide a head start in understanding some of the nightly processing our Psyches perform. If we have a sense of the thrust of the message, we can take a closer look at what's unfolding in our waking life and respond from a hopefully wiser perspective.

In the next chapter we'll learn more about the nature of symbols and symbolic language.

Julie Loar

CHAPTER NINE

Symbols: The Soul's Language:
Three Types of Symbols

*I must learn that the dregs of my thoughts, my dreams, are the speech
of my soul. I must carry them in my heart, and go back and forth over
them in my mind, like the words of the person dearest to me.*

Dreams are the guiding words of the soul.

~ C. G. Jung, *The Red Book*

A symbol is a representation, mark, or image that stands for
something else. Symbols are generally graphic or pictorial emblems
for concepts or ideas. All communication or transmission of ideas takes
place through symbols. Numbers are symbols that represent quantities.
Language is symbolic and is a set of learned symbols, words formed
from letters that are arranged into a grammar. Words are also symbols,
either sounds or written characters, that have been carved in stone,
painted on walls, written on a page, or typed into a computer. We learn
to recognize, speak, or write them to communicate.

Spoken words are concepts that have been turned into sounds. Writing
is the symbolic representation of sounds, images, and concepts. Scholars
believe all writing evolved from pictures, images that represented the
object, through pictographs, ideograms and complex glyphs, into the
alphabets of languages. The word alphabet comes from the Greek
combination of Alpha and Beta, the first two letters of that alphabet,
which in turn came from the earlier Hebrew, Aleph and Beth, which
had in turn evolved from Egyptian hieroglyphics.

In a religious context, a cross has become the symbol for Christianity, a six-pointed star for Judaism, and a star in a crescent represents Islam. The Om represents Hinduism and an eight-spoked wheel symbolizes Buddhism. The phases of the Moon, waxing crescent, full and waning crescent, shaped like a crown, is the ancient symbol of the Goddess. A red rose or a heart often symbolizes love, and a white dove represents peace. A wedding ring is a symbol of commitment, and a crown is a symbol of royalty.

Musical notations represent sounds of a particular frequency, and a dollar sign indicates currency. An arrow with the point on top means "up" and with the point on the bottom means "down." A black circle with diagonal line across the middle says "No . . . smoking, entrance, etc., "fill in the blank. In America a bright red octagon means "stop." Male or female figures on public restroom doors indicate which gender should use the room.

Symbols are how we communicate whether through an inviting smile, a finger to our lips asking for silence, or through the words of the most exquisite prose. Symbols are perhaps the most enduring and fascinating characteristic of humanity. Pictures and images are shorthand for ideas that demonstrate concepts that might take pages of words to explain. The famous expression "A picture is worth a thousand words," attributed to advertiser Henrik Ibsen, makes the point perfectly.

Written language is what separates us from the animals, although they also communicate through sounds, gestures, and movements. Wolves howl to communicate across long distances and this is especially important where their territories are large. A wolf's howl can communicate location, warnings about predators, and information for the hunt.

Coco the gorilla learned to communicate through American Sign Language, ASL, and shared complex feelings with her trainer, including grief when her kitten died. Dolphins communicate through clicks and whistles. Scientists believe this is a highly developed spoken language with all the features present in human language, indicating a high level of intelligence. Sadly, we have yet to crack the code. An African grey parrot named Alex had a vocabulary of 600 words and amazing cognitive abilities. At 31 years of age Alex's last words to his human partner were, "I love you. Be good. See you tomorrow." It's a humbling reminder to be aware of our human arrogance.

Seen this way, the vocabulary of the Soul's language is formed of symbolic images, and the "grammar" is like our own mythology. To access our deeper wisdom and guidance this language must be learned and fluency achieved. Openness of mind and heart are necessary to achieve maximum benefit. Becoming fluent in the Soul's symbolic language sheds light on our path, enhances life's meaning, and reveals our next steps. And when working with dreams, Ted Denmark, PhD, has remarked, "Symbolic interpretation is the algebra of dreaming"— algebra uses substitution of symbols for exact values that give wider meaning.

In her book, *Glamour, A World Problem* (1950), Alice A. Bailey remarked, "There are many ways in which the intuition can be drawn into activity, and one of the most useful and potent is the study and interpretation of symbols. Symbols are the outer and visible forms of the inner spiritual realities, and when facility in discovering the reality behind any specific form has been gained, that very fact will indicate the awakening of the intuition."

Dreams, like other great teachers, often speak in parables or allegories, which are symbolic stories. These stories and their symbolic content must be translated or decoded as they do not appear as "rational" thoughts but as symbols. Dreams speak to us in the timeless language of symbols. Sometimes there are multiple levels of meaning. Dream symbols are a silent and potent language that reaches our self-conscious awareness through the agency of para-consciousness, rising on wings of spirit from the deepest parts of our being as messengers.

While words are an imperfect means of communication that are written or spoken in many different languages, pictures are potentially perfect to convey an idea without words. Jungian author James Hillman has written, "When I ask, 'Where is my soul, how do I meet it, what does it want now?' the answer is, turn to your images." Here he primarily means dreams and art, since both speak a visual language.

Three Primary Types of Symbols

There are three categories of symbols that appear in dreams. We recognize many symbols but dreamwork also requires learning our own symbolic language. Sometimes "signs" are described as something perceived by waking consciousness and the senses, while "symbols" arise from the deeper levels of the Psyche. Having a better understanding of a symbol's personal significance enhances our interpretation of a particular dream. In order to understand the message, we have to break the "code" that our own Psyche has created.

Universal Symbol – A universal symbol contains the intrinsic meaning of the symbol itself. This type of symbol is said to be recognized by everyone regardless of culture, language, or creed. A smile is a universal symbol of good will, a beckoning hand is welcoming, hands held up palm out means do not approach. "X marks the spot," is an ancient emblem of a cross road or "making your mark," and was used like a signature when most people were illiterate.

Numbers are an example of universal symbols even if we don't usually use them in their symbolic sense. While the number one represents a quantity of one, it also connotes the qualitative notion of singleness, being first or alone, and unity. These qualities are intrinsic to the nature of one. Two likewise is a quantity but also signifies the quality of a pair, duality, polarity, attraction, and opposition. Some common meanings of numbers appear in Chapter 16. Certain geometric shapes function as universal symbols. A circle shows both potential and a closed and continuous system. A triangle pointing upward implies spiritual aspiration and hierarchy, a square signifies stability, and displays a well-grounded balance.

Cultural Symbol – Cultural symbols, sometimes called collective, are recognized by groups of people. Examples include flags of nations, colloquialisms, or slang such as the currently popular idiomatic expression "cool," clan plaids, and royal family crests. Sports team names like Rams, Bulls, Cowboys, and Eagles are cultural symbols as are state flowers. The American eagle, Chinese dragon, or Russian bear are cultural symbols of countries. Corporate logos and trademarks, like the world-recognized icons of Apple Corporation, the Golden Arches of McDonalds, or the mouse ears of the Walt Disney empire, are also cultural symbols.

We can now add the plethora of emojis to the list of cultural symbols. Holiday icons such as Cupid's heart, Halloween pumpkin, Thanksgiving turkey, or a Christmas tree, are recognized without words. A four-leaf clover is a cultural sign of good luck since they're rare.

It's always vital to examine the context of any dream symbol as these concepts are relative and, while recognized by a group, might have different meanings to individuals. Sometimes a good omen in one culture may be bad news in another context. Owls and serpents are good examples as they often represent wisdom and seeing in the dark, but in other cultures owls are omens of death and serpents are seen as creatures of temptation.

Personal Symbol – A personal symbol has meaning to one person, evoking emotions and unique responses. A person's son or daughter will represent something very personal. Dreaming of parents, a high school teacher, or a past lover, can invoke specific meaning. If someone works at Disney World or Apple Corporation, the symbol, while cultural, will also take on a personal significance. One person may have a fascination with spiders, creatively spinning webs, while another person may have an irrational fear of arachnids. Another person may feel uncomfortable with wide open spaces while someone else struggles with claustrophobia or a fear of heights.

Dreaming of circumstances that make us feel uncomfortable or happy can indicate how current life circumstances are affecting us. Feelings about the dream symbols can reveal what they are trying to communicate.

✿　✿　✿

My husband has asked why the Psyche doesn't offer clearer dream symbols. It's a serious question when embarking upon dream work and reminded me of something Dr. Marie Louise von Franz said: "The unconscious doesn't waste much spit telling you what you already know." If dreams are sometimes difficult to comprehend, it is because we need to understand that dreams express themselves through symbols—the language of para-consciousness. Of symbols Jung wrote: "A symbol is the best possible formulation of relatively unknown psychic content." He also wrote, "the dream is a spontaneous self-portrayal, in symbolic form, of the actual situation in the unconscious." *The Collected Works of C.G. Jung, Volume 8.*

I have come to realize that to decode dream symbolism we have to fully engage with the process in much the same way we have to really listen to the people in our lives to hear what they say and grasp what they mean. We must be willing to pay attention, do the work and face the truth. We need to learn our own symbolic language, which seems foreign at first and takes time.

Dream symbols are not superficial—we need to go deep. This requires suiting up and getting into the game instead of staying on the sidelines. When we pay attention, and especially when we are open and willing to change and grow, miraculous guidance appears. Therefore, in the context of guidance from dreams or synchronicities, we should ask ourselves what attitude the message or symbolic information we're receiving, is trying to send to reestablish equilibrium in our Psyche.

Para-consciousness provides input to our self-conscious state where self-consciousness may be missing the mark, or in denial, leading to lack of balance. If the self-conscious mind is not dealing with the consequences of our life choices and responses, para-consciousness raises the issues in dream symbolism through the guidance of the Soul. What isn't addressed in waking life arises in dreams so there is an opportunity to do a course correction and bring our Psyche back into balance. Sometimes there are long-term patterns and beliefs that need to change.

In a metaphorical sense all of life can be experienced as a symbolic reflection, offering wisdom and growth. Integrating these ancient and powerful methods of symbolic communication provides enhanced ability to decode messages from our Soul, aiding our spiritual path. Humans are creatures of choice, and therefore we can choose to ignore the signals that come gently, and sometimes forcefully, from the inner reaches of existence. I believe ignoring these messengers can be a great loss of opportunity.

Next, we'll explore other types of dreams and what are described as dreamlike experiences. Our para-conscious journeys in many different realms.

Julie Loar

CHAPTER TEN

Other Types of Dreams & Dreamlike Experiences

*Yet it is in our idleness, in our dreams, that the
submerged truth sometimes comes to the top.*

·· Virginia Woolf, *A Room of One's Own*

Besides the three main types of dreams and the eight basic dream motifs, there are other types of experiences that occur such as nightmares, lucid dreams, and prophetic dreams. Some people have had dream experiences that seem to clearly be related to past lives, and other dreamers have encountered each other while both were dreaming. These experiences add to the complex and rich nature of the Psyche.

Nightmares

Like a big dream, a nightmare is often a profound message, which can be interpreted symbolically like more typical dreams. A nightmare engenders intense and powerful emotions such as fear, anger, guilt, and grief, but the most common feelings are crippling anxiety or disabling terror. A nightmare may wake us, screaming perhaps, in the middle of the night. Nightmares are characterized by sudden awakening with a sense of confusion or disorientation and with a feeling of impending harm and vivid recall. Because of the frightening nature of nightmare images, the dream tends to remain with us through the day, inviting deeper interpretation.

Nightmares can be an important part of psychological work, facing what dwells in the darkness, or unacknowledged parts of the Psyche. As we move into more light, walking our spiritual path, dreams might seem to get "darker" and shadows more pronounced, but it is likely to be only a temporary reversal. Brighter light casts deeper shadows so we can see what we need to learn to bring our Psyche back into equilibrium. Some cultures believe nightmares are important harbingers of coming events.

Venturing into the realm of little-known myth in ancient Greek stories, we encounter a female Pegasus. Aganippe, "the mare who destroys mercifully," was an earlier mythic horse with black wings. Her mane was entwined with Gorgon snakes, indicating her symbolic relationship to the goddess Medusa and feminine wisdom. This was one of the titles of the goddess Demeter as a crone goddess. Aganippe was said to visit as a night time messenger, taking dreamers on flights of fancy. She is the origin of the Night Mare.

Pegasus, the winged steed who carried heroes across the sky in mythical episodes, had his origin in earlier goddess myths. He sprang from the blood of serpent-haired Medusa when the hero Perseus cut off her head. The "wise blood" of Medusa had origins in the principle of *medha*, an Indo-European word for feminine wisdom. Demeter's aspect of Night-Mare/Aganippe may also be linked to the magic lunar horse, Anion, whom Hercules (Heracles) once rode. Some ancient Pegasus legends were associated with the sacred king, or heroic journey to heaven, representing an image of death and apotheosis, which means becoming divine. These powerful myths, and the nighttime horseback journeys they represent, indicate the importance of what can be difficult material to address.

Nightmares often contain subject matter that can be difficult to manage on a conscious level, as in the case of severe trauma. Many people experience nightmares after suffering a traumatic event such as surgery, death of a loved one, an accident, or devastation such as fires or violent storms. The nightmares of combat veterans also fall into this category. In these cases, the content of the nightmare is directly related to battlefield trauma and the disturbing dreams recur until healing takes place. Nightmares are an attempt to balance the Psyche, but therapy is often required to bring trauma to a place of healing.

Wakeup Call

Nightmares not related to trauma generally occur when we have ignored the subtle symbolic communication from our dream guidance and require a more dramatic statement. The main message of a nightmare is "pay attention." Nightmares often contain themes of survival and we are admonished to see the truth. Sometimes these messages relate to health or physical symptoms we are ignoring. Human nature often stubbornly resists change, so a nightmare can act like a shock treatment, dramatically capturing our attention, and framing where we need to "wake up" in stark relief. Decoding the symbols in the nightmare reveal where in our body/mind the warning is pointing.

One dreamer, a two-pack-per-day smoker, reported a vivid dream of having inoperable lung cancer. In the dream state he looked at an ominous shadow on his chest X-Ray, realizing that his entire right lung was infiltrated. He experienced incredible anguish, knowing his life would soon end, and he would never see his children grow up. None of this would have happened if he had quit smoking. When he woke he felt surprise, relief, and joy; he felt reborn. Fortunately, the dream galvanized him to quit cigarettes, changing his life for the better.

When we wake from a so-called "bad dream" the tendency is to want to go back to sleep. That's the very thing a nightmare is trying to prevent. It's a bit like unplugging an annoying smoke alarm in the belief that it's defective, rather than looking for the fire. Nightmares can function as early warning systems, revealing behavior patterns or imbalances in our life that may be leading to disaster. These disturbing dreams vary in theme but the most prevalent is being chased by an unknown assailant. Children usually dream of being chased by frightening animals while adults are often pursued by a threatening figure. Although the encounter may seem unwelcome, this type of dream may in fact have the greatest potential to change our lives if the message is heeded.

Although there isn't a hard and fast answer to dealing with the complex issue of nightmares, and those that arise from devastating trauma take much more care and work, a rule of thumb can be applied. Whatever it takes to discharge and release the lingering emotions of the dream, and examine our waking life to determine where this same feeling emerges, will help release what needs to be healed. Emotions are revealed through the dream setting, and "naming" what causes us to be afraid identifies the source of concern in waking life. Psychologically this is called associative logic; the dream "associates" to our waking life, sometimes to a past event, through a specific emotion. Identify the emotion, locate this feeling in waking life, and healing can begin.

From the standpoint of the spiritual aspirant there is a great irony in the phenomenon of nightmares. Namely, the more horrifying and disturbing the dream imagery the greater the potential seems to be for increased understanding and creative power for change. Like a magical steed who will carry us to the heights of heaven, Night Mares can be our most profound blessings in disguise. The choice is up to us whether we saddle up and face our fear or go back to sleep.

Lucid Dreams

Lucid dreams occur when you're aware that you're dreaming while in the dream state. The veil between waking and sleeping thins, and you are able to recognize your thoughts and emotions as the dream is happening. Some dreamers are even able to influence what happens and change the story, including the people and the setting. Lucid dreams can be so vivid that when you wake you feel certain they really happened. These dreams may leave you shaken and questioning your view of reality.

In Eastern thought, cultivating the ability to be aware you are dreaming, awake in the dream, is central to the ancient Indian Hindu practice of Yoga *Nidra* and the Tibetan Buddhist practice of dream Yoga mentioned earlier. Cultivating this awareness was common practice among early Buddhists. In the book, *The Tibetan Yogas of Dream and Sleep*, author Tenzin Wangal, who is a current teacher in the Bon tradition and founder and director of the Ligminche Institute, says "If we cannot carry our practice into sleep, if we lose ourselves every night, what chance to do we have to be aware when death comes?" Learning to change the dream in progress could help reduce anxiety and transform a nightmare into something less fearful.

Early references to lucid dreaming are also found in ancient Greek texts. Aristotle wrote, "Often when one is asleep, something in consciousness declares something that then presents itself as a dream." The physician Galen of Pergamon used lucid dreams as a form of therapy. A letter written by Saint Augustine of Hippos in 415 CE tells the story of a dreamer, Doctor Gennadius, and makes a reference to lucid dreaming.

Shared Dreams

The potency of a disaster or a significant historical event, seems to stir the depths of collective consciousness. When President Kennedy was assassinated in 1963 numerous people reported dreaming of the incident in advance. Therapists have reported numerous dreams about the virus, illness, and death during the current COVID-19 pandemic as this book is being written in 2020.

Sometimes dreamers share a dream where experiences occur at the same time and the same symbols appear in the memory of the both dreamers upon awakening. A compelling example occurred while I was writing *Tarot & Dream Interpretation*. At the time I belonged to a small group that met weekly to work on their dream symbols. We grew to know each other well and shared deeply and honestly.

These dreams occurred during the time of the 9/11 tragedy. The tremendous loss of life that resulted from the attack on the World Trade Center, and the Pentagon on September 11, 2001, provided another example of collective precognitive dreaming.

Dream A: Many Colored Masks – Dreamer A (me) is in a very large rectangular room without any chairs where many people are standing around looking confused. They seem to be waiting for a lecture. Dreamer A is with her husband and recognizes that the woman who will speak is her fellow dream group member (Dreamer B), who is about to give a lecture on symbols. Hundreds of people of different races and nationalities are speaking many different languages. The lecturer draws symbols on a large dry-erase, white board on an easel. The symbols seem similar to Reiki symbols, like graphic representations of something, which perhaps transcend the language barrier. Each symbol has a specific meaning.

The wall behind the lecturer is covered with masks. Each mask is a single solid color, but there are masks of many different colors hanging on the walls. The masks have very pronounced features and seem to be made of something like Papier Mache. The ceiling area is very brightly lit, and Dreamer A looks up to discover the source of the strong and brilliant white light coming from above.

Dream B: Blue Mask – Dreamer B (another member of the group) is in a very large complex, having just completed some sort of work, and is heading into an enormous public restroom. Her left arm is filled with work papers, lecture notes, and a black binder. She holds a blue mask in her right hand. The mask fits over her hand up to the elbow, somewhat like a hand puppet. The mask is sky blue and has very pronounced features and a pointed nose. The features are sharp and angular. It seems to be made of Papier Mache.

In the dream it is near Halloween, and Dreamer B tries to put on the blue mask. She realizes she can't put the mask over her head or on her face; it is too small. She decides to carry it. She has a strong sense of preparing for something related to costumes. The room is enormous, rectangular, and the ceiling area is enveloped in very bright light. Dreamer B looks up to determine the source of the brilliant, white light, coming from above. There are no chairs in the room, and people are all standing, hundreds, maybe thousands, looking confused.

These dreams shared several identical symbols. Both dreamed of colored masks and large rectangular rooms with brilliant overhead light. In both dreams people were standing because there was no place to sit. Both dreamers mentioned lectures. Dreamer A (me) was aware of Dreamer B in her experience, and one dream seems to begin where the other leaves off. Dreamer A felt the colored masks were symbols of our transitory human personalities that are worn like masks during life and must be laid aside after death, and that the variety of colors represented the numerous nations represented at the World Trade Center. The use of symbols in the "lecture" may have been a way to communicate ideas without words.

Dreamer A – Because I recognized my friend, Dreamer B, in the dream state, I was sufficiently impacted to phone her in the morning. We were surprised by the many similar elements in our dreams. These dreams occurred close to the September 11, 2001, attacks on the World Trade Center where people from many places in the world who spoke numerous languages worked. After working with the dream symbols, we felt these dreams were fragments of memories of actual soul travel and work, helping victims of sudden and traumatic death to make their transitions "into the white light."

This shared experience is unique in my life but reveals the depth of experience that can occur while our body rests and our soul continues to work. Never underestimate the power of your dreams. These dreamers felt blessed to recall their experience and to rededicate themselves to dreamtime service.

Past Life Dreams

Reincarnation is a belief in many spiritual traditions, including what was revealed through the trance work of Dr. Michael Newton and psychic Edgar Cayce, shared earlier. Most relationships, except perhaps the most casual, may well be reconnections with people we have been associated with in past lives. For deep and intimate relationships, such as family, we come back together repeatedly out of both love and karmic necessity.

A special category of dreams seems to be actual past life memories, or night time reliving of scenes from earlier times, which are permanently recorded in what are called the Akashic Records. These dreams have a unique quality and tend to stand out in our mind when we wake with a different intensity. These dreams are characterized by a vividness of detail and sensation that does not fade over time and can be recalled and described years later in all their vivid intensity. Some researchers believe they are actually memories of past life experiences, existing outside of ordinary time. These dream experience may be a type of lucid dream as the dreamer is sometimes able to move about through choice in the dream.

Details such as the landscape or locale are intensified so that we remember the setting more easily. Frequently a language is spoken that we don't know in this lifetime but which we understand perfectly in the past life dream. We may hear ourselves speaking French or Greek. Likewise, the clothes we wear and notice on others would seem like period costumes except they fit perfectly within the temporal context of the dream.

Dream memories of past lives are accompanied by sensations different from other dreams. The dreamer is often aware that they are seeing one or more past lives. These dreams can change the dreamer's attitude toward death and dying as there is a certainty that the person has lived before and that life and death are a continuum.

When a past life dream occurs it usually relates to a karmic issue being dealt in the present waking life. The same players will appear in the dream although relationships may be different. For example, your mother in this lifetime may have been your daughter in another time. In this example the dream dynamics would be played out between you as mother with your earlier daughter. Perhaps the same issues still exist.

Past life dreams usually pack a powerful emotional punch. They are typically triggered by an event in the present that has the same karmic pattern and reveals the need to heal a recurring theme that has been reverberating through centuries or millennia. When these dreams occur, there is a chance to see the dynamic and deconstruct the pattern once and for all.

Memories of a Tsar

The following story is a truly remarkable account of reincarnation and Donald Norsic's book reads like a spy thriller. I have shared five of his numerous past life dreams as short excerpts. I have chosen only a few that are a striking examples of past life dreams and a Soul's journey through space-time. As a result of these dreams and other startling experiences, Norsic had extensive past life regression therapy that led to his recognition of his past life as Tsar Nicolas II of Russia. These experiences caused him to write his truly amazing book, *To Save Russia: The Reincarnation of Nicholas II*, by Donald Norsic, published in 1998.

July 10, 1989 – Vyborg Fortress

"I dreamed about the fortress at Vyborg. I dreamed that an inscription was carved in stone over the mail portal. I saw something to the effect that "All who defend this place shall be blessed."

Prior to this dream Norsic said he knew nothing about this place other than it existed. The fortress is 75 miles north of St. Petersburg, and in Tsar Nicholas' time was on the Finnish side of the Gulf of Finland. During Nicholas' reign he and his family spent part of every summer cruising those waters in the Standart (imperial Russian yacht). As this city is a port, it is highly likely they visited more than once. Norsic says, "History records that there is a fortress there that dates back to the 1200s, and since Nicholas was interested in history, this place was certain to have held a special attraction."

April 5, 1999 – Royal Visit

"I dreamed I was Nicholas with no sense of Donald Norsic. In the dream I was preoccupied with the visit of a prince from another country who was interested in seeing the various departments of government functioning. He was very concerned, having brought his young son with him, that his son would be allowed to accompany him on the tour. In the midst of this I was informed that my daughters were in the process of visiting the cathedral. I had a feeling of gratitude that they were doing this of their own volition, and that they also were agreeable to the performance of their duties to the dynasty."

October 11/12, 1999 – Facial Hair

"In the middle of the night I had a 'Nicholas' dream where I had no sense of Donald Norsic. I was only Nicholas and I thought as Nicholas. I was in the throes of deciding what my facial appearance should be; what facial hair, and how it should look. Up until then I only had a moustache. (Nicholas grew a beard shortly before becoming Tsar, so this past life memory would have been as a youth.) I was also aware in the dream that I was criticized for being too formal in social situations. I responded that "How can I be more casual when I am speaking with the Queen of a nation?'"

February 13, 2008

"This morning I had the first "murder" nightmare since my decision in 1980 to leave the lights on while I slept. This dream happened with the lights on and in the morning. I dreamed I was in the murder situation, that there were others with me who would also be killed. I was not aware they were my family. I was only aware that a man was standing right in front of me, holding a revolver that was aimed at my face; he was intending to shoot. Seconds went by and no shooting occurred, but I knew it was inevitable, I either said aloud or thought, 'You may shoot me in the head but you are not going to shoot me in the face.' I turned my head sideways. As soon as I did that I woke terrified."

December 29, 2020

"I dreamed that I was in old, pre-revolutionary Russia. All I remember of this dream, hours after waking, is that I was partaking in the grandeur of a gala party being given in a noble palace. There were many, many guests present, richly attired, all standing in groups and moving about. The guests were attended by servants who were dressed in 18th century costumes with white stockings from the knees down, white powdered wigs, and great coats made of lustrous pastel satins with long tails in back and double rows of buttons down the front. The servants carried large silver trays; both hands held C-shaped handles on either side. The trays contained elegantly prepared *hors d' oeuvres*, which they offered to the guests. It was a sumptuous affair.

(*Norsic speculated that it was the Youssoupov Moika Palace where the fabulously wealthy Youssoupovs hosted such occasions for as many as 2,000 people. He states that he had never seen a photo of such an occasion to have influenced such a dream).

Prophetic dreams

Since ancient times, precognition has been associated with trance and dream states, as well as waking feelings of premonition. Aristotle conducted what he called a "skeptical inquiry" into allegedly prophetic dreams in his work, *On Divination in Sleep*. He reluctantly accepted that "it is quite conceivable that some dreams could be tokens and causes of future events."

Many parapsychologists believe that precognition, telepathy, and clairvoyance are real phenomena. In the 1960s, ESP experiments were carried out in the sleep laboratory of New York's Maimonides Medical Center. Some of the studies investigated precognition, where the subject described dreams that occurred before the target picture had been selected. Five out of eight experiments were direct hits, and two more were close matches – with odds against of five thousand to one.

Many people experience prophetic dreams, and they can take the form of warning messages, decisions to be made, or direction and guidance. Several historical people have experienced dreams that they believed to be warnings that they were to die.

In J. W. Dunne's 1930s bestseller, *An Experiment with Time*, he related a story of someone who dreamed of meeting a woman in a garden who was wearing a striped blouse, and in the dream, suspected her of being a German spy. Two days later the dreamer visited a country hotel where she was told of a woman staying there who other residents believed to be a spy. She later encountered the woman outside and discovered that the garden and the pattern on the blouse exactly matched her dream.

As mentioned in an earlier chapter, Samuel Taylor Coleridge wrote down *Kubla Khan* when he woke from an opium-influenced dream. In a preface to the work, he described how the poem came to him fully formed in his dream. When he woke, he immediately wrote down the poem but was interrupted by a visitor and could not remember the final lines. For this reason, the poem remained unpublished for many years. Paul McCartney of the Beatles claimed to have dreamed the melody to the famous song *Yesterday*. When he woke, he thought it was just a vague memory of a song he heard when he was younger. Thankfully, he realized it was his own melody and the song was recorded, becoming the most-covered popular song.

New York lawyer Isaac Frauenthal had a dream before boarding the Titanic. "It seemed to me I was on a big steamship that suddenly crashed into something and began to go down." He had the dream again when on board the Titanic and was alerted to the danger when he heard about the iceberg collision. Frauenthal survived the sinking.

Three days prior to his assassination, president Abraham Lincoln told his wife and a few close friends about a dream that turned out to foreshadow his death. According to the recollection of his loyal friend and confidant Ward Hill Lamon, Lincoln dreamed of "the subdued sobs of mourners." Walking from room to room he noticed a corpse lying on a raised bier that supported a coffin in the White House East Room. In the dream Lincoln asked a soldier standing guard "Who is dead in the White House?" The soldier replied, "The President. He was killed by an assassin." Shocked, Lincoln jumped out of bed on April 11, 1865. Three days after his vivid nightmare, Lincoln was shot dead at point blank range by the assassin John Wilkes Booth. We can only speculate how history might have changed if Lincoln had been able to take adequate precautions.

According to Roman historians, Julius Caesar's murder was foretold. The night before his assassination, his wife Calpurnia dreamed that Caesar had been stabbed and lay dying in her arms. In the morning, she begged him not to go to the Senate as planned, and moved by her distress and entreaties, he resolved not to go. But Decimus Junious Brutus, one of Caesar's closest friends, who was secretly one of the conspirators, came to the house and persuaded Caesar to ignore the omens.

Mary Shelley's *Frankenstein* was inspired by a dream. She wrote, "I saw the pale student of unhallowed arts kneeling beside the thing he had put together. I saw the hideous phantasm of a man stretched out, and then, on the working of some powerful engine, show signs of life, and stir with an uneasy, half-vital motion. Frightful must it be; for supremely frightful would be the effect of any human endeavor to mock the stupendous Creator of the world."

In 1845 Elias Howe saw the idea for the sewing machine in a dream. He puzzled over the idea of a machine with a needle that would go through a piece of cloth, but couldn't figure out exactly how it would work. Then he dreamed that cannibals were preparing to cook him; they were dancing around a fire, waving spears. Howe noticed that there was a small hole through the shaft at the head of the spear, and the image of the up-and-down motion of the spears with the hole remained with him when he woke. The idea of passing the thread through the needle close to the point, not at the other end, was a major innovation in making mechanical sewing possible.

Director James Cameron reported that the title character in *The Terminator* was inspired by a dream he had while under the influence of a soaring fever. He dreamed of a gleaming figure of doom emerging from fire; a metallic, skeletal monster with a fixed grin and burning red eyes, dragging itself across the floor with kitchen knives. Cameron said, "I was sick and dead broke in Rome with a fever of 102, doing the final cut of *Piraha II*. Perhaps the fever brought on the dream of *The Terminator* character."

Out-of-Body-Experiences

According to people who have had the Out-of-Body-Experience, a so-called OBE, the experience differs from lucid dreams in the sense that the dreamer is "free" of the body and can actually move about at will and experience things the sleeping person could not. In some cases, people who were under anesthesia had OBEs where they could hear and remember the discussion of the operating team as they watched the surgery with detached objectivity. They may have traveled to other locations in the hospital and overheard the conversation of a loved one. In a lucid dream, described earlier, the dreamer would still be limited to the "ordinary" input and activity of the location of the dream landscape.

An Out-of-Body-Experience in the dream state might be recalled as traveling to a loved one's home, having a conversation where information was gathered, and returning home to bed. In some cases, the information was confirmed the next day, and in some instances, the person who was visited had their own recollection of the nighttime visitation.

Four Seasons Tarot Spread – a dream gift

While writing *Tarot & Dream Interpretation*, which was published in 2003, a book about using Tarot to aid in dream interpretation, I had a remarkable dream. In what has been my long-term pattern of self-doubt, I worried that I would not be up to the task of finishing the book as well as I hoped. I experienced performance anxiety.

The next morning, I woke in pre-dawn hours, realizing I had been given a new Tarot spread in the dream. In the dream I cast a Tarot spread that was familiar in a beautiful and inspiring setting accompanied by my dog Baron. I rose quickly and wrote down the dream, feeling an enormous sense of gratitude and encouragement. I quickly sketched the spread on note paper as the layout had been very familiar to me in the dream but was unknown to me in waking life. I called the spread Four Seasons. The arrangement (shown below) was four cards in a cross, like the four seasons, with a fifth card in the middle that represented Earth and the central issue.

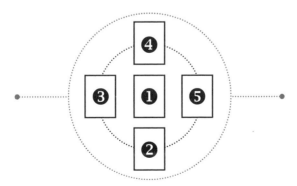

I had already written the Tarot card interpretations that would be used in the book, so I cast the new Tarot spread exactly as I had in my dream, and as I hoped readers of *Tarot & Dream Interpretation* would do, to interpret their dreams. The dream and the Tarot spread were stunning gifts that I vividly and gratefully remember. This dream was a Big Dream for sure. I use this spread whenever I feel timing is part of a question.

This chapter has demonstrated how rich and diverse our dream experiences can be, but our waking life can also be charmed by moments of unexpected grace. We will explore that idea in the next chapter, which discusses synchronicity and serendipity.

CHAPTER ELEVEN

Synchronicity & Serendipity

An event seen only as a coincidence,
rather than a moment of profound grace,
loses the opportunity for transformation.

~ Dr. Deepak Chopra, MD

If we receive guidance from our Soul in dreams, why shouldn't we also receive guidance in waking consciousness since our Psyche is a unity? If so, how do we recognize these messages? The story of the golden scarab, told in Chapter 1, was a quintessential synchronicity experience. A real synchronicity is accompanied by powerful feelings of significance and meaning. It seems that receiving guidance in the waking state requires a bit of a shock to penetrate ordinary awareness and get our attention. Synchronicity or serendipity form the shock—like stepping into an alternate reality—into a waking dream.

These experiences serve to tune our waking consciousness to receive signals and messages and to consciously connect with guidance that comes from our Soul through para-consciousness. It's like a two-way radio where we have to push "talk" when we want to speak, and press "listen" when we need to be in receiving mode. Once the connection is working the radio is "on," the channel is open, and we begin to receive clear signals. This improves as we heed the signs and pay attention.

How do we recognize guidance when it comes, and how is that voice different from our own thoughts? Some people report confirmation, or recognition of guidance, through chills, a sensation in the solar plexus, or a certainty in the pit of the stomach, a so-called "gut reaction." Each person has built-in internal radar that reveals this sense of recognition and rightness. Some see a pinpoint of sparkling light, or hear a ringing in one ear. Some sense a presence or get a rush of energy.

Our attention might be drawn to words on a sign, or to a specific article or book that seems to leap off the page or shelf. The appearance of the numbers 11:11 on a clock or phone is a signal to listen for guidance, or pay attention, waiting for a "message." Overhearing words in a conversation may trigger an insight or sudden realization.

Sometimes the answer becomes clear in the present moment, but at other times we must wait for events to unfold. Sometimes a choice is involved to move the energy forward. Various responses and sensations may also accompany such synchronicities.

Synchronicities

Once on a long flight I fell asleep and had a complicated dream where a wise and advanced teacher gave me a talisman. She said I could bring the gift into the physical realm to remind me of my connection to my guidance. The object was like a sacred object made of shells and feathers. The experience was powerful. The next day, while shopping in a famous book and gift store in Hollywood, I saw the very object in a glass case. Stunned by the synchronicity, I purchased the beautiful piece and still honor that memory. That was three decades ago, but I still remember the experience vividly, and the lovely object remains in a place of honor, reminding me of my connection. During the same visit to the bookstore a yoga book fell on my head from a top shelf, opening to a page that led me to resume my vegetarian lifestyle.

Dr. Deepak Chopra has called synchronicity a "conspiracy of improbabilities." That's a lovely way to view the idea since the word conspire means "to breathe together." He further says, "An event of synchronicity catapults us into a state of expanded awareness. We shift into a heightened frequency or vibration beyond ego where we realize, if only temporarily, that something very significant has occurred."

In his book, *The Celestine Vision: Living the New Spiritual Awareness*, bestselling author James Redfield relates a fascinating story about Dr. Chopra and how he changed life direction.

> Deepak Chopra, a leading advocate of the new mind/body medicine, talks about a series of experiences that led him to seriously consider alternative medical approaches. Until then he had practiced medicine as a traditional Western MD and held prestigious positions at Harvard and other universities as a professor of immunology. Then his life began to change. During a trip to deliver a lecture he was invited to visit with an Eastern leader of meditation, who suggested he study Ayurvedic medicine, an Eastern approach that focuses on the prevention of disease. Deepak dismissed the idea, wanting nothing to do with any approach that sounded mystical.
>
> After the meeting he drove to the airport where to his surprise he ran into an old friend from medical school. In the course of their conversation this friend pulled out a copy of the basic text of Ayurvedic medicine and commented that he thought Chopra would find it interesting. Overwhelmed by the coincidence, Deepak read the book, recognized that to champion this medical approach was his destiny, and went on to pursue his career of popularizing alternative medicine around the world.

Gregg Levoy, author of the bestselling book, *Callings, Finding and Following an Authentic Life*, was once a reporter for the Cincinnati Enquirer but heard a repeating "call" to become a freelance writer. He continued to ignore this summons for financial reasons—too risky. Then a synchronicity radically shifted his perspective. In his article, *Synchronicities: A Sure Sign You're on the Right Path*, written for *Psychology Today* (December 2017) he described what happened.

I was driving home from work one day, listening to a song called *Desperado* by the Eagles, and as I pulled up to the curb in front of my house the last line I heard was "Don't you draw the Queen of Diamonds, she'll beat you if she's able; the Queen of Hearts is always your best bet." I turned off the ignition, opened the door, stepped my foot onto the curb, and there at my left foot was a playing card—the Queen of Hearts. I was utterly dumbfounded, wondering, of course, what it meant.

When I mentioned the incident to a friend that evening, she said, with an extravagant quality of assuredness, that when you're on the right path the universe winks and nods from time to time to let you know. She also said that once you start noticing these little cosmic cairns, once you understand that you're on a path, you'll begin to see them everywhere.

In an October 2019 article titled, *See Your Life Signals Sometimes Via Synchronicity*, published on the web site *www.SayitBetter.com*, author Kare Anderson related a truly remarkable story.

The evening of March 1, 1950 in Beatrice, Nebraska, fifteen members of the church choir prepared to arrive for practice at the church at 7:30 PM. The minister, his wife, and their daughter were delayed when his wife decided to re-iron the daughter's dress. One member took longer than expected to finish his sales report; another couldn't get her car started; two others lingered to hear the end of an especially involving radio program; a mother and daughter were delayed when the daughter came home late from babysitting; and so on.

Ten separate and quite unconnected reasons for fifteen responsible people meant that all would be late that one night. Fortunately, none of them arrived on time at 7:30 PM because at 7:35 a furnace explosion destroyed the church building. Mathematician Warren Weaver recounted the story in his book, *Lady Luck: The Theory of Probability*, calculating the staggering odds against chance for this uncanny event as about one in a million.

In another fascinating account Dr. Lawrence LeShan was researching a book he was writing on mysticism. He consulted with his colleague Dr. Nina Ridenour, and she offered several points of advice, including understanding the differences between Western and Eastern mysticism. She recommended the book, *The Vision of Asia,* by Crammer-Bing. LeShan searched for the book but was unable to find it at two specialized libraries. Then, while walking home, he felt compelled to take a somewhat different route. As he stood at a corner waiting for the traffic light to change, he looked to the ground and saw a book and picked it up. The book was *The Vision of Asia* (excerpted and adapted from the article, *More Amazing Coincidences,* by Stephen Wagner, March 2017, from the website www.liveabout.com)

French poet Emile Deschamps told a fascinating story in his 1805 memoir. He was once treated to plum pudding by a stranger named Monsieur de Fontgibu. Ten years later, the writer encountered plum pudding on the menu in a Paris restaurant. When he ordered the dessert, the waiter told him that the last dish had already been served to another customer, who turned out to be none other than de Fontgibu. Many years later, in 1832, Deschamps was at dinner and once again ordered plum pudding. He recalled the earlier incident and told his friends that the only thing missing to make the story complete was de Fontgibu. At the same moment, the now elderly de Fontgibu entered the room, having gotten the wrong address. (Deschamps, Emile. 1872–74. *Œuvres Complètes*: Tomes I–VI, Reimpr. de l'ed. de Paris. Wikipedia).

The famous psychic Uri Geller had the experience of seeing the same numbers on clocks, hotel rooms, microwave ovens, and other places— particularly 11:11. He found the repeated 11:11 experience so compelling that he wrote an article on his website. He was shocked when he received hundreds of emails from people who were having the same experience and thought this was only happening to them.

Perhaps you are one of the many thousands of people around the world who have noticed that you are drawn to look at the clock, your wrist watch, or cell phone as the digits line up to 11:11. The experience happens so often to so many people that it cannot be dismissed as mere coincidence. I have also had this experience with 11:11 and 444, as well as the numbers 111, 222, 333, and 555. I always feel as if I am being tapped on my shoulder by an angel and pause as if to receive a message.

While I was working on this chapter my husband had a remarkable synchronicity experience related to a scarab beetle, which of course holds a special symbolic place in this book. His account is below. As Dr. Choprah says, these are moments of profound grace when our ordinary state of mind is transformed and we know something miraculous has just occurred. What if these occurrences are not really miraculous but only rare because we do not expect them?

Julie and I had both read, and been impressed by, a famous case cited by C.G. Jung in his vast commentaries on memorable client interactions, involving a golden Egyptian scarab beetle that mysteriously appeared in the window of his consulting studio during a time when said client interview happened to mention a dream sequence involving such a beetle.

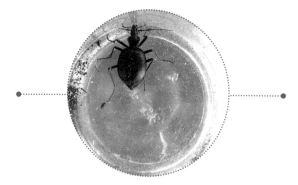

While Julie was working on this chapter, we were discussing the Jung synchronicity phenomenon, her noting the vaunted scarab beetle imagery in ancient Egyptian iconography, and me remembering not only the tumble-bug beetles that I used to watch as a kid—and that had also greatly amused my grandfather—but also the time when she saw one of our local beetles in the kitchen pantry. We remarked that it was too bad we hadn't written the story then because neither of us remembered the incident as well as we would have liked.

Later that afternoon, I went out into the north corner yard where I was building a rock wall with concrete landscaping blocks. I was pulling out scrub holly vines by the roots where the next block was going to be fitted in place when … my attention was drawn to a large black beetle crawling out of the dirt in front of me (!). Of course, I marveled at the sight and immediately thought of Julie and our earlier time of finding such a beetle in the house—which we had been discussing earlier that very day. This was clearly an amazing synchronicity, so I carefully picked up the disrupted beetle in my glove and went into the shop to get a small glass jar so I could take a cell phone picture.

(Note: I can't resist adding that Ted intuitively placed the beetle on a round object, making his image resemble the Egyptian scarab with the rising Sun, And, in hindsight, the appearance of the beetle as Ted was building "seven stone steps" at the end of April foreshadowed the powerful dream I would have later at the beginning of August that became a central key to this book. Only through connecting the symbolic dots as they appeared in the rear-view mirror could I see how the pattern would connect. Adding another layer of synchronicity, my original encounter with the beetle was outside of a window, *just like Jung*.)

Serendipity

Serendipity is often called a "happy accident" and is seen to be an occurrence or development of events that occur by "chance" in a beneficial way. Serendipity comes from *Serendip*, an old name for Sri Lanka (Ceylon), called *Sarandib* by Arab traders. The word has been exported into many other languages with the general meaning of "unexpected discovery" or "fortunate chance." The first acknowledged use of the word in English was by Horace Walpole in 1754 in a letter he wrote to his friend Horace Mann. Walpole described an unexpected discovery he had made about a lost painting of Bianca Cappello by Giorgio Vasari, referencing a Persian fairy tale, *The Three Princes of Serendip*. The princes were "always making discoveries, by accidents and sagacity, of things they were not in quest of."

Once while driving into town, I had an experience I will never forget. I stopped at a red light at an intersection and was first of a line of cars. As the light turned green and I prepared to drive ahead, I heard a loud and authoritative voice say "Wait!" I was so startled I did not accelerate to proceed with my left turn. Within a few seconds a car hurtled through the intersection at a high rate of speed and drove off the road on the other side. I was shaken as I realized had I proceed through the green light the vehicle that ran the red light would have struck me broadside with disastrous consequences. Whose voice did I hear? I believe the power of the Psyche through para-consciousness, produced an audible voice that prevented a tragedy. In this case the serendipity was a happy non-accident.

Serendipity often applies to inventions that were made by "chance" rather than intention. Andrew Smith, editor of *The Oxford Companion to American Food and Drink*, has speculated that most everyday products had serendipitous roots. He said that many early discoveries were related to animals. For example, he suggested that the origin of cheese possibly came from the nomadic practice of storing milk in the stomach of a dead camel that mixed rennet from the stomach with the milk.

Other remarkable examples of serendipity in inventions include:

The Post-it Note™ was created after 3M scientist Spencer Silver produced a weak adhesive, and a colleague used it to keep temporary bookmarks in a church hymnal.

Silly Putty™ came from a failed attempt at making synthetic rubber.

The microwave oven emerged when Raytheon scientist Percy Spencer noticed that emissions from radar equipment melted candy in his pocket.

The Velcro™ hook-and-loop fastener resulted from a bird hunting trip when George de Mestral looked under a microscope at the cockleburs stuck to his pants and saw that each burr was covered with tiny hooks.

Penicillin was discovered by Sir Alexander Fleming when he returned from vacation to discover a Petri dish that contained a staphylococcus culture had been infected by a Penicillin mold and no bacteria grew near the culture.

How do we find the meaning and receive the gift as a galvanizing energy to move us forward? Dreams offer most of the symbolic messages we receive, but as we engage the unseen and our guidance, a reciprocity occurs. Then, the symbols begin to synchronize with our waking awareness, creating synchronicities and serendipities that grab our attention in powerful ways.

One way to work with guidance is to view life as both a waking dream and a sleeping dream where symbolic content is always available. This creates a mechanism for our guidance to speak to us continually and provide feedback regarding the ongoing lessons in our life. In a sense we begin to experience life in a shamanic state of awareness, or in a quantum reality, and the potential to receive messages is dramatically increased. We know that it is all connected; we just can't see the big picture that reveals the linkages and symbolic triggers that vibrate the nexus.

When we view life as a waking dream, we pay closer attention to what appears in our path. Indians who live according to their traditions do this as a matter of course, and the characteristics of certain animals are taught and remembered. In the same way we might study dream symbolism and learn our own responses to certain people or creatures from our night time dreams, we stop to analyze what the objects that show up during the day might be saying.

For example, a bird may land right next to you on a fence post. What kind of bird is it? What is the bird doing? Some other animal may literally cross your path. How does the creature make you feel? You may overhear a conversation at the market, or someone may make a remark that stops you in your tracks, because it's the exact answer to a question you've been pondering. You may be driving on the highway and a truck passes you with a word painted on the side that sends a specific message. A particular song lyric may play in a context that has meaning for you. A friend may say something in a certain way and you "know" it is a message.

Usually there is a feeling in your body that announces that this is not just a random event but is instead a symbol. Some people get a chill, others experience some sensation in the solar plexus. Knowing your own unique bodily reaction will become familiar to you, and as you open to your waking dream, it will become clear what your own signal response is.

It's my experience that when people start to live life this way what shows up does so with startling clarity. The author Jack Kornfield has said, "Those who are awake are in a constant state of amazement." This is precisely true for those who learn to work with life as a waking dream. Prepare to be amazed.

In the next chapter we'll take a deep dive into dreamwork and examine tools and techniques to improve your experience.

Part Three

Signposts & Milestones

*The spiritual journey involves going beyond hope and fear,
stepping into unknown territory, continually moving forward.
The most important aspect of the spiritual path
may be to just keep moving.*

~ Pema Chodron, Buddhist teacher

CHAPTER TWELVE

Getting Started: Learning to See in the Dark

When you're ready to work with your dreams,
your dreams will work with you.

~ Ted Denmark, PhD

As explored in Chapter 5, we are accustomed to considering our waking life, self-consciousness, as the "real world." Until we are awake spiritually, we live mostly in the realm of the self-conscious mind, our current lifetime's personality, and our daily external lives. Because the physical world has material substance this is where we focus most of our attention. Dr. Marie-Louise von Franz has explained that there are two levels of reality--the psychological inner world, with its dreams and myths, which she insisted was as real as the outer world of our waking experiences, and the outer world of the senses.

Seen this way, our dream state is as real as our waking state—perhaps more real in some ways—because of the connection to meta-consciousness. We are in closer contact with eternity, and as our self-conscious mind is silenced during sleep, we can open to guidance from higher levels of our Psyche that come through our para-conscious. Those who have worked seriously with dreams know this to be true.

Once we realize we are on a long journey of many lifetimes, and are in possession of the map, we can work with our dreams, synchronicities, and serendipities in a more intentional way to hear our Soul's voice and have para-consciousness help guide our way. Ancient wisdom has provided the map and the journey's goal; dreams can act like a torch and compass, lighting the way, and pointing us in the right direction.

In the same way that our awareness of the Path of Initiation is veiled in the modern world, it is likewise difficult to find teachers, unless we look in the pages of classic books. I have written this book because I believe we can learn to become our own oracles, listening to the guidance that comes from within and "above." My premise is we can learn to form, or strengthen, a conscious connection with meta-consciousness, our Soul, and our spirit Guide, and by learning the language of symbols, the language para-consciousness speaks, we can be guided in the journey of life.

Central to spiritual work is formulating ideals to which we can aspire, and these ideals become the central focus of our dream work. Since most traditions agree that para-consciousness is more attuned to our Soul, our job is to learn to understand the language of dreams, becoming receptive to guidance from Spirit.

Working with dreams requires commitment, but even a small amount of time is an investment that pays large dividends in insight and growth. Learning from our dreams is not an abstract process as there is no real separation between our waking life and dreamtime, although different aspects of our Psyche, just like brain waves, are "dominant" at different times. Our consciousness is a unity that expresses as phases along a continuum.

Dreams and synchronicities provide feedback to change mental attitudes, beliefs, and behaviors that are held in waking self-consciousness, which if accepted and acted upon, can restore equilibrium. This creates the field of potential for growth and development. Of course, we must first be willing to face what can sometimes be difficult material that is hidden in shadowed places. We must make a plan to improve and heal. Albert Einstein is credited with saying "Repeating the same behavior and expecting a different result is a form of insanity."

Although guidance flows from meta-consciousness to para-consciousness, and from that level to waking self-consciousness, through dreams, synchronicities, and serendipity, we are still mostly unaware of how the Psyche functions and instead look outside for answers and guidance. However, when the self-conscious mind awakens to the realm of Spirit and connects to guidance, a powerful flow from para-consciousness informs our choices, improving and accelerating growth. As noted earlier, for a long time the process is automatic and unconscious. When our spiritual growth reaches a certain point, we become aware of our Soul and the feedback loop takes on more power. Then the energy flows freely between the aspects of our Psyche, and our lives partake of magic and miracles.

This connection aids us on the Path as we do our work and learn our lessons. We make healthier choices at the physical, mental, and spiritual levels, and over lifetimes, the result is what has been termed a Soul-infused personality (see diagram in Chapter 7, page 135). At this stage of our growth, when a conscious connection is made to meta-consciousness, our Soul is able to infuse our waking self-consciousness with more light and wisdom. I suspect this knowledge may be the origin of the idea of being "born again."

We learned in Chapter 6 that Dr. Michael Newton's clients reported that each Soul has a Spirit Guide, an advanced being who remains with the evolving Soul throughout all the incarnations from "birth" as a new Soul until "graduation" when the growing and evolving being has progressed through the rainbow color spectrum of Souls described in Chapter 7. Our Spirit Guides, like guardian angels, remain with us on the long journey as our Souls move through their own long development from innocence to enlightenment. This idea aligns with what is taught in Theosophy, and the books of Alice A. Bailey, about the Solar Angel, a being of great love and wisdom who watches over our reincarnating aspect like a guardian, or a mother with a child, through the ages-long journey.

When the memory of a dream remains upon waking, it's worth spending time to capture the essence and the main symbols, even if brief and somewhat skeletal. When a dream stays with us, providing much stronger potential meaning, I believe our Soul has stepped into the process and sends symbolic content that ups the ante of significance. And when we embark upon a conscious spiritual path the potential for more input from the level of our Higher Self increases. I believe this is what I have experienced writing this book and was what I didn't really understand before. And when we are experiencing a crisis, or trying to solve a difficult problem, it is likely that dreams will be more striking and have the potential to impart wise counsel through their symbols.

Learning discernment, and drawing meaning from symbols that present themselves as either waking synchronicities or sleeping dreams, is part of the spiritual path. Symbols will be covered in the next Chapter and also in Chapters 14-18. We must be willing to do the work, humble enough to accept the guidance received, and courageous enough to take the necessary corrective action in our beliefs and behaviors in waking life.

Dr. Meredith Sabini, PhD, of the Dream Institute in Berkeley, California, has said, "There are many kinds of dreams and many purposes to dreaming: to review the past, reflect on the present, rehearse for the future." In her dream consultation work she listens together with the dreamer, for themes in the storyline of the dream. She says she looks for the questions embedded in the narrative to translate the symbolic language.

What appears in a dream should not be a replacement for good judgment, abdication of personal responsibility, or reduced to a parlor game. Dream messages are intended to restore balance to the Psyche and promote growth. No matter how skilled and insightful another person's analysis, You, the dreamer, are the ultimate authority where meaning is concerned. It is your dream; books and experts are only guides, and what is important is learning how your Soul, your Higher Self, meta-consciousness speaks to you.

Ancient wisdom traditions have valued messages in dreams for thousands of years, and now modern science emphasizes about the critical importance of sleep and dreams. What is missing from modern science and psychology is how to bridge ancient ways of knowing with cutting edge science. How does paying more attention to our dreams, and learning the Soul's symbolic language, fit into the larger picture of spiritual growth? I've had several powerful dreams and other experiences that seemed to point the way.

Dramatic Dreams

It's clear that few dreams merit intense study and analysis, but when one arrives with stunning intensity, and a feeling of significance, I pay attention. I wrote in the Introduction that I had such a powerful dream in mid-March 2020 that I titled *Messenger Bag*. That dream admonished me that I was not paying attention to my "work," and the startling image and message in the dream called me to create the two-volume *Sky Lore Anthology*. And it was interesting to be reminded through that dream symbol that my first book, published in 1997, was titled *Messengers*. That's an example of how dream symbols connect over time. This dream is interpreted in Chapter 13.

Two months later, as I began work on this book, and doubted myself, I had another startling dream I called *Elephant Takes a Leap*. In that dream a huge golden elephant jumped across a large crevasse— a seemingly impossible feat. The golden elephant gave me the courage and impetus to proceed, propelling me into deeper work, and counseling me not to give up. Through the sometimes challenging process of writing this book, the golden elephant has inspired and encouraged me. These dreams are among those interpreted in Chapter 13.

No true heroic quest is without tests and trials—it's simply the nature of the Path. So, it was not surprising that the demon of doubt raised its head again three months later, casting a dark shadow over what was now months of work. Once again, I struggled, doubting myself and the value of this book, wondering if I was on track and even questioning the book's existence. Those moments of crippling doubt seem to come during a deep creative process as if to test our resolve. Searching for confirmation, as I went to bed I asked for a "sign," or an answer, as I have suggested readers do in their own process, either in a dream or as a synchronicity.

My Soul answered, and early the next morning I woke from a dream with a strong central symbol, which I titled *Seven Stone Steps*. The dream and subsequent synchronicities did indeed give me a sign. When I began working with the dream in the way I've developed over many years, I realized in a flash of insight that the title I gave the dream, *Seven Stone Steps*, held the conceptual frame of a process I had used for decades with both dreams and synchronicities but had never "named" or formalized. I quickly wrote down the steps as the guidance flowed through me. As a result of the dream, and the gift of awareness, I have called the process *Seven Steps in Dreamwork*©.

The experience of *Seven Stone Steps* included a dream, a gift in the dream, and a synchronicity the next day. This was as powerful for me as the golden scarab story described in Chapter 2. I was awed and humbled, and I hope the *Seven Steps in Dreamwork*© process described at the end of this section will be useful for others.

Aware that something truly remarkable had just occurred I knew this dream and its gift were profound examples of how guidance operates in our lives and would bear careful study. The dream became like a case study for the work, and I have since used the process to work on my own dreams while writing this book. An amazing journey of guidance and grace has unfolded.

I have interpreted the *Seven Stone Steps* dream in detail as one of the examples in the next chapter. Given the power of the experience, and the subject matter of this book, I have spent a lot of time with this particular dream as it feels like a multi-layered set of keys that will continue to unlock understanding and provide counsel on deep patterns in my life. Few dreams deserve this in-depth analysis, but sometimes a dream is filled with so many layers of meaning that it is worthy of this amount of time and attention. When we commit to this work we receive profound dreams, and other dreams are often brief but pithy commentary on our growth progress.

I worked on the *Seven Steps in Dreamwork©* process as I hope readers will on your own journeys. Then in mid-October, two and a half months later, as I was getting close to finishing the first draft of the book, I had another riveting dream. That dream further changed the game, showing me that I was not only writing a book about dream work and symbolism, but I was also being worked on myself. I titled that dream *Light on the Lake.* That dream caused me to adapt and revise my concept, showing through a dramatic experience how dream guidance develops over time.

A short form, a Quick View of the *Seven Steps in Dreamwork©*, follows on the next page and is meant to be a one-page overview of the process. Following that is a step-by-step explanation and suggestions of how to work with the process. This basic template can be used with both dreams and synchronicities, wherever a symbol or symbolic experience occurs. However, the most important thing is just writing down, or typing, the dream so you can listen to your own counsel. The forms and instructions can be downloaded from *www.SatiamaPublishing.com* or *www.JulieLoar.com*

Seven Steps in Dreamwork

Dream Diary Quick View

A step-by-step method to interpret your dreams so they become a powerhouse for understanding and growth.

TITLE _____

DATE _____   TIME _____

Record

1 **Record:** Write down the beginning, middle, and ending scenes in present tense. Notice and record your primary feeling(s) when you wake. (Use additional sheets if needed.)

2 **Symbols:** Highlight symbols throughout the dream.

3 **Title:** Choose a title based on the main symbol.

4 **Picture:** Find an image/picture or make a sketch that represents the main symbol / title.

Reflect

5 **Current Conditions:** What is happening in your life right now that frames the issue? What problem are you trying to solve?

6 **Core Issue:** Interpret the dream symbols. Identify an ongoing pattern or limiting belief. (Use additional sheets if needed.)

Resolve

7 **Change Required:** What step can you take that begins to deconstruct a limiting pattern or belief and create more conscious harmony? Make a plan, take a step or an action, even if it seems small.

Julie Loar
Ancient Wisdom for the Modern World

Record

STEP 1 – Record

Write down the beginning, middle, and ending scenes in present tense. Notice and record your primary feeling(s) when you wake.

(Download the *Dream Diary* worksheet from *www.julieloar.com* or *www.satiamapublishing.com* or set up your own blank diary to begin.)

Recording your dream is the most important step, even if you go no further. When you wake and remember a dream—just get the words down. The first, and probably most important thing, to notice are your feeling(s). This is a big clue to the dream's message. Feelings are powerful indicators in dreams, and the nature of a feeling or a strong thought upon waking can sometimes reveal the whole thrust of the dream's significance. What emotion did you feel when you woke? Fear? Joy? Anger?

Taking time to record the dream (or synchronicity) communicates to your para-consciousness, and your Soul, that you are receptive to guidance and serious about improving. This receptivity and commitment invite synchronicities and serendipities and opens a channel for more symbolic messages. When synchronicities connect to a dream, this links the dream world with the waking state, and para-consciousness speaks directly to our self-conscious waking aspect.

Note all the details you remember when describing the scenes— lighting, setting, characters, feelings, colors, textures, sensations, numbers, clothing, and time of day, or time period in history. Some may seem subtle, unimportant, or even confusing. Don't judge; just write or type and capture as much as you can remember.

A surprising fact has emerged from dream research, which is the importance of recording the dream in the present tense. For example, "I am walking through the upper level of a house," rather than "I walked through the house." Research has shown that relating the dream in present tense, as if it's happening right now, brings the story to life and aids recall. Present tense also keeps the feelings active.

Psychologist Fritz Perls discovered that present tense captures the alpha brain wave pattern of the dream, enhancing recollection and aiding interpretation and synthesis. Other research indicates that shifting to past tense may indicate an unconscious attempt to distance from potent emotional content. Relating the dream in present tense appears to enhance the flow of information from para-consciousness.

It's also valuable to record the date and time as looking back later over a series of dreams it is possible to perceive recurring symbols and messages that yield powerful insights. In hindsight we may also see how events in waking life are connected to dream contents. When we start to really pay attention, deep psychological patterns, and Shadow material, are revealed, and we can realize what needs to change.

Dreams have a basic structure, like acts in a play, and tend to happen in beginning, middle, and ending scenes. This can be helpful to organize the content. At first, you might only remember the end of the dream, but as you write down the dream story (or type on the computer keyboard), recall improves and images and visions reappear in your mind the way the dream originally happened. And, like a story, the next scene expands the "plot" and builds tension, raising the stakes. The final scene either shows a result or leaves the dream unresolved. Sometimes only one scene remains in memory, along with one or a few symbols. That's okay, work with what you have. Often more will surface later.

STEP 2 – Symbols

Highlight predominant symbols: people, setting, places, objects, time of day, and period in history.

Using a colored highlighting marker, or the highlighting function in your word processing program, highlight the symbols—the people, places, and things . . . the "nouns." You can also underline and use **bold** type to emphasize the symbols as I will do when I relate the important dreams and symbols that shaped this book. Those emphasized symbols stimulate your intuition. Some symbols may seem subtle, unimportant, or even confusing at first. Don't judge at this stage. In Step Six you will investigate and interpret the hints and images, including the meaning of animals, buildings, houses, objects, actions, roads, paths, weather, season. What symbol stands out the most? This is a clue, or identifier, to the dream's main message and to the dream's title.

Notice any recurring symbols or themes and make a note in your *Personal Symbol Dictionary* (see Chapter 19 Tools and Techniques for more). Over time you will recognize certain symbols and how they fit into limiting mental patterns or belief systems that your dreams are helping you realize and deconstruct. Usually, the most significant symbols in dreams are the people, animals, houses, buildings, or vehicles.

STEP 3 – Title

Name the dream; this brings the dream's central theme or message into sharp focus.

One symbol usually stands out from the rest in either a dream or a synchronicity. Choose this image to represent the dream and use this as the title. Giving the dream a title is powerful and draws the focus to the main symbol or central theme and message. Once chosen, the title seems to cause everything else to line up around the main symbol and the name you've given to your dream story.

Later, when you recall a dream's title, the core message comes through. The rest of the symbols support the main message, like a supporting cast in a movie. Be sure to place the record in your *Dream Diary* so you can observe how guidance develops over time. There are more suggestions in Chapter 19, which has more Tools and Techniques.

STEP 4 – Pictures

Choose an image or make a sketch that represents the dream's main symbol and the title. This creates a strong visual link.

Find an ***image*** or ***picture*** that represents the title and depicts what you feel is the central symbol. You might find something online or have a photo that fits. Some dreamers like to do their own sketch. When I had the dream I titled *Messenger Bag*, I found a picture of a messenger bag to place in my *Dream Diary*. When I look at the image, I can see and feel all the work and worth the bag contains and the message the dream communicated that I should value what's inside. When I look at the picture I feel a sense of confirmation that what I symbolically carry in that bag, and my work, have worth and deserve attention.

If you are working with a synchronicity, a central image will also appear, like the golden scarab story with Dr. Jung's patient, or the Queen of Hearts playing card in the writer's story told in Chapter 12. Using an image as part of your recording is a powerful tool. This brings the message into even sharper focus and seems to turn on the intuition like a switch, opening a communication channel to para-consciousness in the waking state—like stepping across a threshold. Even the search for the picture or image can shed light on the dream's meaning. Don't underestimate this step.

Reflect

STEP 5 – Current Conditions

Describe what is happening in your waking life right now that frames the issue.

This step brings you into the psychological realm, revealing where the Psyche needs to return to a state of equilibrium. The conscious mind is where we make our choices and get our consequences in waking life. In the same way that poor choices in waking life can lead to conflict or physical illness, shown by pain and other symptoms, other choices, or trauma, can lead to psychological imbalance.

Conflict and pain are direct feedback mechanisms, and so are dream symbols and synchronicities. We can look to where we feel emotional pain to locate the source of what is out of balance. Dreams, through the agency of para-consciousness, reveal what is out of balance and what needs to change. If you are honestly working on growth, knowing what is happening in waking life presents the Current Conditions. Where are you out of alignment?

Think about what happened yesterday, or recently, that is the issue or challenge you are facing. Did you have another argument with your spouse? Did your boss give you a negative review? Are you worrying about money? Were you offered a promotion that involves a big move? These are obvious examples but show how to place the dream symbols within the significance and context of waking life and how your wise self is suggesting what you might need to shift or change. Dreams are commentary on present circumstances and strongly held mental patterns.

You, the dreamer, are the only one who can provide this most critical element. Dreams always have an antecedent in waking life even if most dream content is routine processing and filing and not meant for deep analysis. When a dream lingers there is usually a strong message to be received.

STEP 6 – Core Issue

Interpret what the symbols mean to you. What core issue, limiting pattern, or psychological mindset do the dream symbols reveal? What needs to change?

After you've done the left-brain work of recording your dream in as much detail as possible, it's time to switch gears. Take a deep breath and open your intuition with intention as you reflect on the meaning. Trust your guidance. Interpret your first intuitive sense and allow your awareness to deepen. Breathing and opening you enter what has been called a field of grace. Remember, you the dreamer are the ultimate authority on meaning. No one dream image can be taken in isolation. Chapters 14-18 provide some symbols and their meanings to get you started. Guides and books can help with questions, but it's your dream—let the symbols speak to you.

Note your primary emotions and first impressions. Look for any patterns or recurring symbols and note this in your *Personal Symbol Dictionary* (described in Chapter 19). Is the dream portraying a theme that repeats in your dreams? Look for puns, word plays, and humor. Para-consciousness loves to teach through humor. Learning to laugh at our foibles is strong medicine for the evolving self.

As you let the symbols speak, the Core Issue, or concentration of mental patterns that the dream is addressing, will arise in your awareness. Breathe deeply again and take it in. Accept that change needs to occur and open your mind and heart to recognize what needs to change. Look for repeating conflict, internal or with others. Left unaddressed, conflict leads ultimately to pain.

Unless the dream is prophetic, or a shared experience, in almost every case the main character, and all the actors in the dream, represent aspects of your nature. Your Psyche is the casting director and everyone represents a quality or behavior you're reflecting on, so if you're not center stage, take a close look at who is. You, the dreamer, are author, actor, and audience—and analyst. Your Soul sets the stage, writes the plot, and casts the characters.

Determine the identity of the main character(s). Like stories, there is a main protagonist who might be the dreamer or someone symbolizing the dream's main issue. Examine the nature and personality of the character in the starring role. What is the age and gender of the main character? How do you feel about the leading lady or man? Who is the hero/heroine, and is there a villain? Are you the star in your story, or are you an observer, watching the action as if it's on a screen? Observing rather than being in the action can indicate emotional distancing from the subject matter being addressed in the dream.

Investigate hints and images, including animals, buildings, houses, objects, actions, roads, paths, weather, seasons. Are you dreaming in black and white or color? Identify the overall tone: harmonious, mischievous, or dangerous. How does it make you feel? What is happening? Who are the people? The time of day and season of year are also clues. Use the information in Chapters 14-18 on symbols; these are just ideas to stimulate your intuition. Does the dream contain symbols that have repeated over time?

Take your time and trust your guidance. You might reflect if you feel this is a feedback or encouragement dream, or even a Big Dream, and think about which symbols seem to be universal, cultural, or personal. How does that affect your thoughts and feelings about the dream and the area of life presented by the dream's symbols? Does this dream fit into one of the main eight common dream themes? If so it's important to notice recurring settings or themes as they reveal aspects of your Core Issues. Look for psychological patterns contained in the symbols that drive your behavior and responses and need to be unpacked.

The nature or quality of the symbols reveal how and what they are trying to communicate. Water is generally said to represent emotions. How the water appears in a dream provides clues to the dream's message. Do you dream of an ocean, and is it calm or stormy? Is the body of water in our dream a clear, mountain lake or a stagnant pool?

Dreaming of an old man rather than a baby may indicate the stage of an enterprise from infancy to completion rather than the individual depicted in the dream. You may dream of a bed, and you may be using this as a symbol, through a play on words, for a situation in your waking life where "you've made your own bed." Perhaps you dream of a church bell, and there is something in your life which just doesn't "ring true."

Resolve

STEP 7 – Change Required

Identify the change, message, realization, or shift in mindset or behavior that needs to occur in your waking life. Make a plan and resolve to take action.

This is the real pay dirt of dream work—the fuel for growth and transformation. This could be a change in attitude, a mental shift, or a course correction. This final step is what will lead to real and lasting change. What has to be outgrown or jettisoned, like the chrysalis of a butterfly, so you can spread your wings and soar to new heights of unique expression?

What adjustment, shift in perspective, new mental attitude, action, or behavior is needed to restore balance and equilibrium in the Psyche? This often requires courage, humility, and radical honesty, but the results are life changing. Examples could be a job change, courage to enter into a relationship, or recognition of the need to forgive someone and move on. Make a plan to take some form of step, no matter how small, to bring your Psyche into equilibrium. Choose courage, not comfort. Then watch the transformation begin to occur in your life.

Sample Questions

We need to learn how to frame the question. This is perhaps the most important stage of the process. The questions below are only suggestions—just a starting point. As you work with this technique you can expand this list with your own questions and keep it handy so you can add to the list whenever a new question enters your mind. Record the responses to these questions in your Dream Diary and observe what happens with your dreams over time. Answers can also come in the form of synchronicities and serendipities.

> What do these symbols mean to me personally?
>
> How am I acting in the dream? Why am I doing this?
>
> Is this an area of ignorance or denial?
>
> What is my current waking state of mind?
>
> What was my state of mind when I went to sleep?
>
> How can I integrate a positive dream message to gain confidence?
>
> If I step back, what scene is portrayed on the "TV" screen in my mind?
>
> Do I feel safe or threatened? Am I running from something or someone?

In the next chapter I will share several important dreams, including the three just mentioned, that I had during the months I wrote this book that have guided and encouraged me throughout this process.

As I worked very consciously with this process the dreams and synchronicities showed me in a concrete manner how the Psyche acts to restore balance and come into equilibrium when we participate at our level of awareness. At every stage I felt a sense of awe, humility, and gratitude.

CHAPTER THIRTEEN

Reading the Signs: Dream Interpretation

A dream that is not interpreted is like a letter that is not read.

~The Talmud

As I described in the Introduction, I woke from a stunning dream in mid-March 2020 and have been writing ever since. Over the course of writing this book I had roughly two dozen dreams that I recalled in the morning, recorded, and worked with—some more than others. There were other dream fragments, but they slipped away as I woke, and maybe only one symbol remained. As significant dreams occurred, at what would later be revealed as critical moments, I faced my Core Issues and did my best to apply what I was learning. Overcoming self-doubt, and gaining courage and confidence, were key to my progress. The journey of the book has been the metaphor for the lessons of my life and the dreams have chronicled the steps.

I believe dreamwork may be the most important activity we can engage in. Knowing our core issues and how they are triggered by life events, shows where the keys are hidden. Dr. Marie-Louise von Franz has counseled, "If we can stay with the tension of opposites long enough —sustain it, be true to it—sometimes we can become vessels within which the divine opposites come together and give birth to a new reality."

Of the dreams I worked with while writing the book, I have chosen seven that have served as signs of encouragement and direct guidance that lifted me up and kept me going; one counseled a course correction. I have also experienced a few stunning synchronicities.

This chapter shares and interprets these dreams with the benefit of hindsight and the ability to see the dreams and synchronicities as sequential puzzle pieces. It's humbling to recognize how deep and debilitating the Core Issue of self-doubt has been in my life. I wouldn't say my hindsight is 20-20 because I am still on the journey and still taking steps on the Path, but the clarity of insight is better, and fluency in the symbolic language of my Soul is much improved.

These dreams guided and inspired me as I wrote this book, and illustrate how the voice of my Soul, meta-consciousness, developed the theme over time and counseled me to adapt. Dreams don't happen in isolation; there is always an antecedent, as well as subsequent symbolism, that builds on the choices for change and growth we make at the self-conscious level. The symbols and messages that came from these dreams and related synchronicities shaped my journey and helped heal my limiting beliefs and mental patterns, which is of course the deeper purpose of the teaching.

I worked with the dreams that follow, using the *Seven Steps in Dreamwork©* process to penetrate their meaning. The *Seven Stone Steps* dream is interpreted first—out of chronological sequence—since that's where the process was revealed. Although I had been using this process for many years I hadn't perceived the structure or the idea of "steps" that this dream offered as a gift in the form of a template.

Over time, and with the clearer vision of hindsight, the symbolic messages changed shape, but the same theme was developing and unfolding. The *Messenger Bag* dream sent a clear message that I should pay attention to my worth and work, and paradoxically the pandemic gave me the creative space to search for my identity.

The consistent image of forgetting my wallet (worth) and ID, my literal identity, repeated in subsequent dreams. These symbols asked hard questions that have haunted my life: Who am I? What is my work? Am I worthy?

The symbols of a messenger bag, toolbox, white briefcase, and black luggage that appeared in the following dreams were symbols of containers for my work that evolved over time. The succession of dreams with developing images illustrated in a powerful way how our dreams can be thematic and symbols can morph over time. Perhaps as you read these dreams you will see clues I missed? In each of the important dreams I carried a bag, box, or suitcase. In two dreams I pulled black roller bags—baggage. What hidden/shadow material might be concealed in those bags that I dragged along and that weighed me down? The shape and style of the containers changed, indicating perhaps my evolving relations to the "work."

Highways and taking steps were also repeating symbols as well as vehicles, representing the journey. In several of the dreams I walked without a "vehicle," on my way to an uncertain destination. As I look back I believe my major insight is the work has its own value and I cannot measure my own worth by external response.

In the dreams that follow I have used **bold** and <u>underline</u> text to emphasize the symbols in the black and white version and yellow highlights in the color version. When I'm ready to place a dream in my *Dream Diary*, I place the Title (Step 3) at the top and the Image (Step 4) beneath the title. Recording the dream is always the first and most important step as you take care to notice the thoughts and feelings that linger as you wake. The title, image, and symbols emerge from the recorded dream.

What follows is my own work with key dreams from this journey and are meant as examples of my own process. Do what works for you. You can create your own form for your *Dream Diary*, mine is an example that works for me and others who have tested it. The form(s) can be downloaded from *www.SatiamaPublishing.com* or *www.JulieLoar.com*

Seven Stone Steps

August 3, 2020 | 7 AM

RECORD

STEPS 1 – 4: *Title, Image, Highlight Symbols*

Beginning Scene: I am walking along a highway on the <u>right side</u> of the road in the same direction as the traffic although no vehicles are present. I don't know why **<u>I do not have a car</u>** – I think my husband has it. I am alone in a <u>**wide-open vista**</u>, a flat landscape with a blue sky, and a vast feeling of <u>**openness and positive potential**</u>. I can see in all directions. I believe it is morning. I am walking to the Early Child Care Center where I volunteer.

Middle Scene: Although it seems like I have a long distance to walk, I quickly arrive at the <u>Center</u> and notice there are <u>**7 new stone steps**</u> on the left side, leading up to the entrance at an angle. The ascent is <u>**left to right**</u>, leading up to the front door, which is wide and glass. It's easy to see inside. The steps are rough-hewn and a natural sand color like Egyptian pyramids. They are arranged in an attractive manner. I admire them and feel grateful as they make my <u>**ascent to the Center**</u> (heart of the matter?) much easier. Before this time there was just a <u>**dirt mound**</u> that was <u>**difficult to climb**</u>.

I easily go up the steps and enter the building. I am surprised that a concert or **performance** is in progress and see many **purple and gold chairs**, facing left (past-unconsciousness). People are sitting and listening to a **classical chamber orchestra**, which strikes me as an odd performance for young children. I notice only adults are in the audience and there seems to be a **celebration**.

Someone greets me. I think it is my friend MC. The Center Director wants me to stay for a meeting on the second floor, but I decline as I only intend to stop by to see the progress of the remodeling. I have another pressing commitment, (to myself?), and a meeting with her at this time feels like a wrong choice and a delay. I get a brief tour of the remodeling progress and take my leave after a polite amount of time. **As I leave I feel proud of my choice not to repeat past behavior of overdoing and overcommitting and leave the Center feeling empowered.**

Ending Scene: I am walking again, **taking steps**, outside in the same wide open and light vista, heading in the same direction as before. Someone drives up beside me (my husband?) and picks me up along the highway in his/my vehicle to drive me to my destination. The vehicle is a **dark-colored SUV, a "utility" vehicle**. I feel that I will arrive on time. I awake feeling very positive and optimistic.

REFLECT

STEPS 5 – 6: *Current Conditions, Core Issue*

STEP 5 – Current Conditions In waking life, I have been unable to connect with the Center Director to go by for a tour and explain in person why I am resigning from the board of this non-profit where I have served for twelve years. My role with this organization has been a decade of struggle but also filled with accomplishment and satisfaction. This center has been under reconstruction and remodeling for two years and will finally open later this month (August 2020).

My role with this organization is coming to an end, making space for other things. For some months I have felt my volunteer obligations were affecting my ability to perform my own work. Resigning is influenced by my dreams.

STEP 6 – Interpret Symbols, Identify Core Issue

Vehicle and Walking: I am walking, needing to advance on foot "by steps" under my own power because someone else has my vehicle. Even though I am walking, I feel free and unencumbered. I am advancing step by step.

Open landscape: A sense of vast potential and openness

Seven stone steps: Angled from left to right—past to future—this is my new direction. The steps were "new" and made my ascent to Center easy; the ascent was a difficult dirt mound before. The number 7 is a spiritual number. In Qabalah, 7 represents victory and a temporary rest. I feel that I will do what is necessary and I will arrive on time if I keep taking the steps. The 7 Steps are the sign I asked for and a powerful gift of dream guidance and synchronicity.

Stone: Traditional symbol of wisdom—the Philosopher's stone

Center: The goal and the heart of the matter; my ability to get to Center was easy

Concert/performance: What I'm creating—leaving on a "high note," classical, seemed to be celebrating; classical chamber orchestra, this "performance" and the book is not for children but adults.

Purple chairs: Purple is said to be a royal and spiritual color. Chairs are facing "left" relative to the front of the building. Performance related to this center is part of the past.

Friend: The person who met and mirrored me is bright and well-educated; she has extensive knowledge but suffers from doubt. She greeted me in the Center and offered me the choice to repeat past behavior. I declined.

Highway of life: I had no anxiety – only positive potential. Proceeding under my own power in beginning, taking steps. I arrive immediately. But at the end my vehicle arrived and took me to my destination "on time."

The dream's symbols indicate that I am taking steps in the right direction and will finish "on time." My feelings were all positive in the dream as well as when I woke. In the dream I chose what felt positive and then was empowered to move ahead.

As I am writing this book, I have been worrying the last couple days that what is written in *Symbol & Synchronicity* isn't really appropriate or won't be of interest. The ongoing Core Issue is lack of confidence and self-doubt. Am I only speaking to myself? Who is the audience? I asked for a "sign," or some sort of confirmation, that my effort is worthwhile. This dream was the answer. What is humbling is how deep the issue has been in my life and the effort required to deconstruct the pattern Another layer is depending on some else and not stepping into my own power.

RESOLVE

STEP 7: *Change Required*

Change Required: What is needed to change to restore equilibrium in my Psyche is more trust and confidence to continue the journey—more faith, less doubt. This is a rare dream for me and one where the main symbol of *Seven Steps* will remain a central image in my life. Because this was such a powerful dream that revealed complex patterns I have deeply mined the rich content, taking the needed time. So, I will need to keep taking steps to build confidence. Just keep taking the steps.

Action: August 10, 2020, I resigned my twelve-year relationship with this non-profit. I will work on this dream in detail, using the *Seven Steps in Dreamwork*© process and create the template to use in the book.

Synchronicity: The next morning, while working on the dream and looking for an image to reflect the title, I discovered a book titled

Seven Stone Steps; the steps on the book cover angled the same way and rise in a similar way to the entrance to a building. *Seven Steps* is also a strong personal symbol of guidance from decades ago as I began my conscious spiritual journey—*Seven Steps* was the title of an introductory course. So, I received a powerful synchronicity as well as the dream.

Messenger Bag

March 19, 2020 | 7 AM MDT

RECORD

STEPS 1 – 4: *Title, Image, Highlight Symbols*

Beginning Scene: I am attending a <u>conference or big meeting</u> like INATS (International New Age Trade Show), a large gathering with lots of <u>exhibits</u>. I don't know if I am there to present, exhibit, or just attend and learn.

Middle Scene: I am sitting at a table with my friend KC. She has a <u>large and delicious cupcake</u> that she pulls from what seems to be a <u>book with lots of pictures.</u> The cupcake looks like Italian cream cake with lots of walnuts. I am <u>not happy with my own lunch</u> and search in the "<u>book</u>" for another cupcake. I do not find anything and when I examine my strange lunch, I am very disappointed. The packaged lunch is inside plastic wrap with five soggy pieces of what had once been white bread, soaked in some sort of greasy brown gravy. There is also a wilted salad. The lunch is <u>neither appetizing nor nutritious</u>. I am <u>hungry</u> and want to <u>get fed</u>.

I decide to <u>go into the exhibit hall in search of something better</u> among the many booths. I walk down a <u>long, wide brightly-lit white hallway</u> that is parallel to the exhibit hall. When I am about 100 yards I realize I don't have any money. I return to get my <u>purse</u>, which is a saddle colored messenger bag. All my <u>work, wallet, and identification</u> are in the bag. Everything of value in my life, <u>past, present, and future</u>, are inside.

My messenger bag is about twelve inches square and <u>stuffed to overflowing with my writing</u> and other work. <u>The bag is really heavy.</u> For some reason the strap isn't visible (or broken?) so I have to <u>carry the bag like a baby</u>. I keep putting the bag down because of the <u>weight</u>. I also keep <u>forgetting the bag and have to search</u>. I finally find the bag and set off again in search of food.

Ending Scene: I am alone, walking in this big event building among the many booths and exhibits, still searching for food and looking for the last place I left my messenger bag.

REFLECT

STEPS 5 – 6: *Current Conditions, Core Issue*

STEP 5 – Current Conditions I woke on this March morning to six inches of snow and blizzard conditions, recalling magical snowy mornings a decade ago when I wrote *Goddesses For Every Day.* I have just been laid off from my part-time editing job because of the pandemic lockdown and suddenly had the much longed for space for a creative effort of my own. I am very worried about money and how I will support myself (get fed?), but I finally have time and space to address my own work.

STEP 6 – Interpret Symbols, Identify Core Issue

Large conference: With many exhibits, learning and displaying my work or attending to learn. This is a recurring symbol over many years. In these dreams I often have to present and feel ill-prepared and doubt myself.

Exhibits: What is on display? What are the many offerings? What is my role?

Food/hunger: Not getting proper nurturing; how do I get "fed?" My friend is getting fed from a book filled with colored pictures. She is just allowing and receiving. Trust.

Long lighted hallway: Positive transition to get my needs met. Need a new way.

Messenger bag: Container of my identity, worth, and life's work that I keep forgetting. It's "heavy," meaning weighty? I need to pay attention and care for myself. Who am I? What is my work? How do I make the work important?

Weight: The work is important, "weighty."

No strap on bag: My work is not supported in a traditional way.

Carry the bag like a baby: Bag contains "precious cargo" and I need to pay attention.

I'm not taking care of my work or paying attention to how I get nourished. The *Core Issue* is a long pattern of self-doubt and working for others for a sense of financial security. Although I was successful in the corporate world, I have been unable to fully support myself with my own work of writing and consulting. I have tried to heal the pattern.

RESOLVE

STEP 7: *Change Required*

Change Required: This dream delivered a strong message to pay attention to my own work, worth, and identity. Because of the pandemic I now have the time. I must symbolically find the messenger bag in my life and honor my work and the identity that work represents. I have also volunteered for non-profits and was feeling exhausted. I perceive that the issue is not black and white, either/or. How to balance security (food) issues with precious creative work.

Action: I resolved to put *Atlantis Rising* articles into books. I had purchased Vellum software to make this possible on my birthday in January; now I had the chance to put that desire into action. Six weeks later I successfully self-published a two-volume set of *Sky Lore Anthology* and then began work on this book. I originally believed this would be a similar compendium of earlier written articles on dreams, but Spirit had other ideas. (Note: March 2021 *Symbol & Synchronicity* is nearly finished. And in Nov. 2020 I contributed to the Nature Conservancy as a way to ground the dream and received a messenger bag at Christmas as a thank you).

Golden Elephant Takes a Leap

April 28, 2020 | circa 6:30 AM

RECORD

STEPS 1 – 4: *Title, Image, Highlight Symbols*

Beginning Scene: I am on the <u>ground floor</u> of a very large <u>grey</u> <u>concrete structure</u> that I think is a <u>parking garage</u>. I am alone and walking through the building, searching for something, probably my <u>vehicle</u>.

Middle Scene: I face one challenge after another as I continually <u>climb to a higher level/floor</u> in this large structure. I keep climbing to higher levels although I think the <u>"way out" must be on the ground floor.</u>

Ending Scene: At the end I am alone and an observer at a distance as a huge <u>golden elephant in clothes, like the Hindu god Ganesh,</u> prepares to jump across a <u>deep chasm</u>. He has a <u>deadline</u> to meet and is on a <u>mission</u>. As I watch I send good thoughts but don't see how he can make it as the distance seems too far. All is <u>darkness</u>, but there is a <u>golden light</u> shining from somewhere. The <u>golden elephant takes the leap</u> and makes it across. The light in the darkness is golden and magical. When I wake I feel inspired.

REFLECT

STEPS 5 – 6: *Current Conditions, Core Issue*

STEP 5 – Current Conditions   I've been working very hard on *Symbol & Synchronicity* and feeling frustrated and doubtful. In the beginning I thought this would be a simple matter of transferring articles on dreams into an e-book. Can I make it? Will it be any good? I am working hard but feeling inadequate. This dream feels as significant to me as the dream I had of my dog Baron in autumn woods where I was gifted a card spread in dream while writing *Tarot & Dream Interpretation*. (That story is told in Chapter 10).

STEP 6 – Interpret Symbols, Identify Core Issue

Ground floor: Start with the basics at the foundation level

Grey concrete structure: Industrial and solid

Parking garage: Temporary vehicle storage; am I looking for mine?

Climb to higher level: I keep going higher

Golden elephant: Elephant was enormous, shining, and golden, dressed like a god. Reminds me of Hindu god Ganesh, who removes the obstacles he creates. In his book *Animal Speak*, Ted Andrews says, "If elephant has come to you, prepare to draw upon the most ancient of wisdom and power. You will have an opportunity to either help yourself or others reclaim your most primordial royalty."

Deadline/mission: There is an assignment and strong sense of purpose

Chasm: What must be faced feels like a daunting challenge

Darkness but golden light: In hindsight I believe this dream foreshadowed the light on lake in a subsequent dream and means I will have the guidance I need and must trust.

Takes the leap: Makes it across; courage and commitment are required

Once again, the **Core Issue** of self-doubt is revealed. I doubt that the elephant can make it, and I am worried for him, which translated to my ability to write this book. I don't think I can "make it" and failure could mean a fatal fall. At this point I had finished the two-volume *Sky Lore Anthology* and felt great satisfaction. *Symbol & Synchronicity* felt like a much different challenge, but also felt like a calling or "assignment." Faith and self-confidence are required as well as just doing the work.

RESOLVE

STEP 7: *Change Required*

Change Required: Substitute a sense of confidence for self-doubt. Watching the elephant leap across a huge crevasse, a seemingly impossible task, sent a clear message that I would have what I needed to write the book. I also knew I could call on that powerful symbol in times of doubt and questioning. Just keep writing and trust the knowledge and answers will come. Ganesh removes the obstacles he creates.

Action: I placed a lovely carved small statue of Ganesh in a prominent place in my office where I can see him every day. I have visualized and called upon the golden elephant many times throughout my journey.

Note: In Hindu tradition, Ganesha is the large **elephant-headed god** who **symbolizes** wisdom, understanding, and a discriminating intellect that one must possess to attain perfection in life. Ganesha is widely revered as the remover of obstacles, the patron of arts and sciences, and the deva of intellect and wisdom. As the **god** of beginnings, he is honored at the start of rites and ceremonies. ... In the *Ganapatya* tradition of Hinduism, Ganesha is the supreme deity. Ganesha holds a "sweet" in his left hand, the jewel of *Sat Chit Ananda*, "truth, awareness, and bliss." His right hand forms the mudra of blessing and protection. He is the adopted son of Lakshmi, the Hindu goddess of wealth and wisdom.

Wooden Toolbox

September 5, 2020 | 7:30 AM

RECORD

STEPS 1 – 4: *Title, Image, Highlight Symbols*

Beginning Scene: I am in a situation of <u>mass evacuation</u>, needing to <u>leave or travel</u> somewhere. I am with my younger daughter and we are attending a <u>trade show</u>. There is a sense of <u>urgency</u>, and I do not have a vehicle and have to walk. There is a sense of <u>leaving destruction behind</u> and heading for a new world. I can only take with me what I can carry. I see an amazing <u>camper or Gypsy caravan</u>. Beautiful and clever. It is turquoise. I am amazed at the amount of work and how beautiful it is, but the camper is not mine to use.

Middle Scene: I am preparing for the journey, gathering what I need and can carry—I need to <u>travel light</u>. I have a sense of staying in <u>temporary quarters</u>, preparing for the larger part of the journey. I sleep in a strange place, like a dormitory. A man, who I think I am traveling with, gifts me with a beautiful, <u>hand-carved wooden box</u> that is the size and shape of a <u>train case</u>, but I think it is meant to be a <u>toolbox</u>. The box is a <u>beige color of wood, polished and sleek</u>. I think it must be pine as it is almost <u>white in color and very light weight</u> for wood. The shape is gently curved—it seems like a <u>work</u>

of art—highly polished and beautiful. I am thrilled with this valuable gift but afraid it will be heavy. I will keep my more precious items in this beautiful box. I already have a black roller bag, a carry-on type of suitcase, for my clothes.

The man (animus?) does not travel with me but gives me a beautiful gift for my journey to hold what I need. I will travel alone into the future.

Ending Scene: I am walking alone with my baggage along a highway. I carry the toolbox in my left hand and pull the black rolling bag in my right hand. An endless line of huge semi-tractor trailers seems to stretch all the way to the horizon; too many to count. I think they are carrying provisions for the future. The trucks are on the left side of the highway, and so am I. It doesn't feel "wrong" so I think I am in a foreign country or unknown land and heading toward an unknown destination. It is still light. The sun is setting in the direction we are headed.

Although I don't have much space to walk on the side of the road, I feel equipped and ready to make the journey, but I feel it will be a long way to my destination. I don't feel I have a choice, I am leaving a dangerous situation, but something that has to be done because of circumstances in the world. I find a place to stop and get free room and board and a safe place for the night. I have a sense that the future has promise but I still have a distance to travel.

REFLECT

STEPS 5 – 6: *Current Conditions, Core Issue*

STEP 5 – Current Conditions I am struggling to find suitable part-time work to support me financially. Once again, I am doubting my ability to finish this book. I am trying to trust. I am receiving unemployment, but it is not enough. The possible jobs I have found are full time and far away. I only get the message "not selected."

STEP 6 – Interpret Symbols, Identify Core Issue

Mass evacuation: Leave the past behind and do it now, sense of urgency

Younger daughter at trade show: Recurring symbol that means learning and displaying; she represents how I need to grow.

Sense of urgency: Take action now; gather what I need

Walking alone: Taking steps under my own power

Travel light: Take only what I need; focus on "light"

Gypsy caravan: Not my transportation but showed how others were preparing. We are amazed at the amount of work and how beautiful and clever the turquoise camper is.

Temporary quarters: Lodging appears when needed

Hand carved wooden box: Container for precious cargo (toolbox not messenger bag). Pine is a light wood and the box is not heavy. Christmas trees can be pine. Pine boughs are decoration. Now have tools instead of carrying heavy work in bag. What will I carry in this priceless gift? My writing materials, wallet, identification.

Black roller bag for clothes: Routine clothing items, my attitudes, are concealed

Well-equipped: I carry what I need and the rest will be provided

Leaving danger: Into safety and a whole new world

Walking on "left" side of road: Past, subconscious, intuition

Huge semi-trucks on left side: Heavily loaded with provisions for future on "left" side of road – foreign country

Ongoing financial fear is the dangerous situation. What are my tools and my precious items? Again, the Core Issue is doubt and worry. This dream says that I have the "tools" and the container to build my new life. I must keep walking in the direction I am headed. I have what I need, and I'm being given room and board and a safe place. There is light on the horizon. I can place my most precious items in the toolbox. Is the toolbox my book or what I need to finish it?

RESOLVE

STEP 7: *Change Required*

Change Required: Counsel is to keep going, just keep taking steps, keep writing. I will have what I need when I need it, and I'm able to carry the most valuable and essential things with me.

Action: Make a list of what I will carry in my tool box of life. What are the most important items and qualities that I will use to craft my evolving self? Most importantly, I am a writer.

White Eyelet Briefcase

September 28, 2020 | 6:00 AM

RECORD

STEPS 1 – 4: *Title, Image, Highlight Symbols*

Beginning Scene: I am at Durango <u>airport</u>, waiting to check into a flight. I think I am going to Dallas to visit my older daughter and granddaughters. I am with TD, KC, and my father. I have a <u>black bag on my right side</u>. I realize I have left my <u>white eyelet briefcase</u> in the car. The briefcase is white cloth, not a very practical for a utilitarian work item, but unique. I go to my car to get the brief case as the bag has my work, wallet, and ID.

Middle Scene: I am ready to check in for my flight and look inside the white briefcase for my <u>wallet</u>, which has my <u>identification and money</u>. When I look inside the wallet is not there. The briefcase is new and I have just transferred items for the trip. My <u>cell phone</u> and <u>makeup bag</u> are there, but no black wallet. The airline representative <u>allows me to check in</u> because of my cell phone where I can prove my identity.

Ending Scene: I go through <u>security</u> and walk down a <u>long lighted hallway</u> toward the <u>departure gate</u>. I worry how I can get <u>new identification</u> for my <u>return trip</u>. (When I woke it occurred to me that in the waking world my husband could FedEx the wallet to me in Texas, but this was a puzzle in the dream of how I would get my new "identification").

REFLECT

STEPS 5 – 6: *Current Conditions, Core Issue*

STEP 5 – Current Conditions   Met with a friend about teaching from material in this book, trying to make a plan to earn money going forward. Still worrying about money, writing, still taking the steps, as the messenger bag morphs into a tool box and now a white fabric briefcase.

STEP 6 – Interpret Symbols, Identify Core Issue

>*Airport:* Travel to new location; flying gives an aerial view and higher perspective

>*Black roller bag:* Like in tool box dream, carried on right side; clothes and basics

>*White briefcase:* Instead of messenger bag and tool box; forgot again—left in car

>*Missing wallet and identification:* Forgot my identity and worth again

Black bag on right: Another black bag with clothes: attitudes are concealed

Cell phone and make up: Communication and external decoration

Security: Go through, out of danger head to gate; transition

Hallway: Brightly lighted transition

Gate: A portal to a "state" where I lived in the past and had financial success

New identification and money: Not a problem when I woke; way ahead is clear

The Core Issue continues to be that I am not enough; insecurity and doubt. The symbol of a bag and box is shifting and morphing, but I still can't find my value, worth, and identity. I am traveling to a place where I had "success." I make it through "security" because of my cell phone, which has my contacts. Am I ever good enough? Who am I and what is my work? Teaching? Consulting? Will anyone want it? The good news is when I wake, I realize I can easily solve the problem. I go through challenges but they are overcome.

RESOLVE
STEP 7: *Change Required*

Change Required: Keep going and finish the book; make a plan. Even without my identity and worth I am able to make the journey. I have what I need, and the challenge could easily be met. Have faith that I have what I need. I am on a journey, and I will have what I need to solve my problems. Need more trust.

Action: Make a plan to finish the book and create a Zoom workshop to teach about the material

Light on the Lake

October 18, 2020 | 6:30 AM

RECORD

STEPS 1 – 4: *Title, Image, Highlight Symbols*

Beginning Scene: <u>I am driving</u> my car beside a large and lovely lake on the right-hand side with my friend KC as passenger. I describe to her my Seven Step process of working with dreams and symbols. The weather is glorious and <u>brilliant light</u> shines and sparkles on the lake. I have a <u>vision of a diagram</u> for the process for the dream book that I have received as guidance.

Middle Scene: I have a <u>strong sense</u> that I need to get it down to remember and to better understand so I can better explain to her. I make a <u>U-turn</u> and turn <u>left</u> into a small <u>parking area</u>. We get out of the car and cross the road to a small <u>rest area</u> with a picnic table. I attempt to translate the vision, the <u>design image</u> to paper. I can see the plan in my mind's eye in black ink on an ivory colored paper. The design is <u>complex and coded</u>, but I feel it is urgent to <u>translate to paper</u>. I take a picture of the very <u>complicated and detailed diagram</u> with my cell phone as the <u>brilliant, sparkling light shines on the lake</u>. I sense it is mid-afternoon, and it is also the season of autumn—three-quarter point.

Ending Scene: We get back in the car to <u>continue on our way</u>. The <u>light</u> in this dream experience is <u>exquisite, shimmering, reflecting off the lake in a magical way</u>. As the dream ends I am looking at the <u>light on the lake, feeling inspired</u>.

REFLECT

STEPS 5 – 6: *Current Conditions, Core Issue*

STEP 5 – Current Conditions   Sent work-in-progress diagrams to TD yesterday and met outside at a picnic table with friends and discussed work. Working on book and diagrams and seven steps for book. Asked for a dream last night. The dream happens in the afternoon, which is similar to the timeframe in the dream of the Tarot spread related in Chapter 10. I originally titled the dream *Dream Diagram*, but I changed the title and image the next morning to *Light on the Lake* as I realized the light was the strongest symbol.

Step 6 – Interpret Symbols, Identify Core Issue

> ***Driving my own vehicle:*** No longer walking, and I am at the wheel.
>
> ***KC in passenger seat:*** Who was also present in Messenger Bag and White Briefcase dreams; fellow student for many years
>
> ***Brilliant light:*** On waters of consciousness – guidance
>
> ***Diagram in vision:*** The image was complex and coded and I knew it was related to the *Seven Steps* process and very complex in the dream; needed to get it down
>
> ***U-turn:*** Go back and look again; modify course or direction
>
> ***Parking area:*** Small, open, and easy contrasted with the huge grey structure in Elephant takes a leap. It's a temporary simple stop.

Picnic table by lake: Not hungry and food is not involved; just an easy place to draw diagram.

Autumn: Three quarters through the process.

This dream feels like I am making real progress on the Core Issue of self-doubt as the light is bright. The guidance is that I should reexamine the *Seven Steps* process to improve and adapt. When I woke I had the sense I needed to clarify and simplify.

RESOLVE

STEP 7: *Change Required*

Change Required: Keep working and trust my guidance—light on the lake is brilliant. Work on the *Seven Steps* process diagram and instructions to make more user-friendly. The message is to take another look. Need to adapt and modify, earlier guidance was not "wrong" but the process needs to be finessed.

Action: Revise the *Seven Steps* process to make more clear and inviting.

Synchronicity – Light: – While working on this dream in the morning, I walked out of my office and saw the Sun shining on the lake across from my home lake in the same way it did in the dream—a stunning synchronicity. The shimmering quality of the light was the same as in the dream and was not a condition I had ever noticed in more than a decade of living in this house.

Reconciliation – Balance Sheet

April 5, 2020 | 6:00 AM

RECORD

STEPS 1 – 4: *Title, Image, Highlight Symbols*

Beginning Scene: I don't recall fully the early part of the dream except that I am working on a <u>large project</u> and it is nearly finished. I have a sense of coming close to a conclusion.

Middle Scene: I have made large <u>deposits of money</u> over a period of time as part of this project and hope that the full balance has been paid. There is an accounting of whatever the balance is, and I learn that I owe what seems to be <u>$11</u>. All the <u>figures/symbols</u> on the balance sheet are the same, looking like stylized elevens. They are <u>bright red-orange</u> symbols that look similar to <u>Chinese characters</u> drawn with a paint brush—<u>symbolic language</u>. They all look like the number <u>11</u> and seemed filled with <u>lots of energy</u>. The balance sheet is divided into squares and these large symbols stretch <u>out of the boxes</u>.

Ending Scene: I look at the <u>balance sheet</u> and the <u>11</u> figures and realize that the figures also resemble the symbol for <u>Gemini</u>. I am very relieved, as although I was hoping for a refund, the balance due is quite small compared to what has already been paid, and **I can easily pay the balance.** I feel relieved and grateful. I wake with a positive feeling.

REFLECT

STEPS 5 – 6: *Current Conditions, Core Issue*

STEP 5 – Current Conditions   I am in the final stages of finishing *Symbol & Synchronicity*, worrying a bit about working with the Vellum software to do the e-book design and final formatting of the book. I have worked on this project for a year and want the book to be the very best of what I'm capable. This has been a daunting effort. The dream gives me a sense of confidence that I can easily manage what is required.

STEP 6 – Interpret Symbols, Identify Core Issue

> *Big project:* The work on this book over a year's time
>
> *Eleven:* Master number of high energy; symbol of Gemini, next month
>
> *Balance sheet:* What remains to be done; what is still owed; the end is in sight
>
> *Chinese looking symbols:* The balance sheet is expressed in symbols
>
> *Red-orange:* Color of Taurus on the color wheel, which begins April 21
>
> *Gemini:* Sign begins May 21; perhaps a timing issue as that's my goal to get the files to the printer.

The Core Issue of ongoing self-doubt is healing and I have nearly accomplished the assignment of this book. I feel a sense of pride, accomplishment, and confidence. The doubt about this project is in the past and I reflect back on the Golden Elephant dream that inspired me to continue. There are final details but I am not overly concerned about the remaining challenge.

RESOLVE

STEP 7: *Change Required*

Change Required: The dream offers powerful encouragement, saying only small balance remains. The symbol of the characters and most of the "investment" already made is like a report card. There is still work that must be finished before Gemini, May 21, but the balance seems small and manageable.

Action: I believe this is the seventh dream I've waited for. This dream has many layers and levels of symbolism. Finish the book and focus on getting it out into the world.

Note from Wikipedia: Chinese characters do not constitute an alphabet; rather, the writing system is "logo syllabic," a character generally represents one syllable of spoken Chinese. A character may be a word on its own or a part of a polysyllabic word. The characters themselves are often composed of parts that may represent physical objects, abstract notions, or pronunciation.

Part Four

Traditional Symbols

*The spiritual journey involves going beyond hope and fear,
stepping into unknown territory, continually moving forward.
The most important aspect of the spiritual path
may be to just keep moving.*

~ Pema Chodron, Buddhist teacher

CHAPTER FOURTEEN

Dream Symbols:
People, Clothing, Settings, Time and Seasons

All the figures in dreams are personified features of the dreamer's
own personality. The dream is a theatre in which the dreamer
is the scene, actor, producer, author, audience, and critic.

~ C. G. Jung, Dreams

What follows in the next five chapters are what might be considered "typical" interpretations and are not meant as answers but rather thought starters to stimulate your intuition. These symbol interpretations are only examples that can stimulate decoding of your own dream symbols. When working with dream symbols, no one image should be taken in isolation. Always examine your thoughts, feelings, and reactions to the symbols in your dreams. For example, as mentioned in an earlier chapter, one person may be fascinated with spiders, while another may be terrified to the point of a phobia. So, a spider appearing in a dream would suggest a very different meaning to those individuals—one might mean creativity and the other could suggest setting a trap.

Our Soul, Higher Self, our meta-conscious, the eternal and wise part of our Psyche, speaks to our conscious waking mind through the agency of para-consciousness. Naturally, we must choose to pay attention. We also have to learn to decode our own symbolic content, and this can take time, like learning a language. An honest examination of our dream symbols can bring deep insights and stunning revelations. The symbols convey meaning as well as what needs to be changed or integrated at the self-conscious level. The effort pays dividends of personal and spiritual growth.

People

Some of the most potent dream symbolism comes in the form of people who appear as actors in our dream dramas. People are usually the most important symbols, and as noted in Jung's quote at the beginning of this chapter, reflect something about us. Meta-consciousness and para-consciousness act like central casting at a movie studio, choosing people we know, such as relatives or family members, or famous people, as actors in our dream dramas. These figures represent personality qualities of character or issues we are confronting. It's easier to accept this idea when we dream of people we admire, but when we have strong negative feelings about someone, we tend to reject the notion that he or she could be acting out a part of us that we are reluctant to face.

The nature of this symbolism can come as a surprise or shock as there may be difficulty understanding why our Psyche chose a particular person, someone we may not like, as a symbolic figure. You may wonder why you would ever dream of "that person." In waking life you might describe that individual as stubborn, inflexible, and unreasonable. Make a note of that as you work with the dream. In this case your wise self could be showing you where you are being stubborn and unreasonable, perhaps projecting that unconscious quality onto someone else in your waking life. The dream actor holds up a symbolic mirror, reflecting a facet of your behavior in a particular setting or situation; look in that mirror with honesty. Reflect on whether the actors and characters in your dreams are familiar figures or persons unknown to you? Analyzing whether we, or the other people, are alone or in a group can reveal our feelings. Is the situation social and relaxing or work related and stressful?

A good technique is to write down three qualities or characteristics of a dream person, like the example just given of 'stubborn and inflexible.'

Do this without stopping to think—free association. The first three attributes that come to mind are usually the most revealing. You might dream of your grandmother, and the three descriptors might be, loving, kind, and generous. Or, you might dream of your boss, and what pops into your self-conscious mind might be rigid, overbearing, and controlling. A famous movie hero might show up in a dream drama and you might describe him as attractive, charismatic, and successful. Perhaps you dream of a friend you haven't seen in years and you describe her as thoughtful, detail-oriented, and precise.

In each of these generic examples your Psyche is choosing people to stand in for an aspect of you in a certain context happening right now in your waking life. What is the current situation where you might need to be more kind and loving? Is there a situation in your life where you might be acting rigid or overbearing? Where might you need to engage some charisma to have more success? And so on. Current Conditions are always of supreme importance as you reflect on what your dream actors are portraying; what is happening right now, maybe just yesterday.

You might dream of being pregnant, or a pregnant woman, if you are gestating a new project, or considering a big change. Caring for an infant can show the early stages of an enterprise, or a change in you that is just beginning to take shape. Likewise, dreaming of a funeral, or the death of someone familiar, may reveal a chapter in your life that is about to close. The qualities of the dying person can reveal the nature of what needs to change or be released. People often dream of the parent of the same gender to represent an older, and hopefully wiser, aspect of themselves. Likewise, dreaming of yourself as a child, especially in your childhood home, can suggest unfinished business or unhealed wounds, or perhaps harken back to simpler and more innocent times. Sometimes an old emotional scar or belief system is still lurking in the Shadow. Dreams prod us to face these buried patterns, bringing the issue to conscious awareness, in order to release the trapped energy.

Sex and Intimacy

People often dream of lovers, real or symbolic. Sometimes the significance has to do with the balance of masculine and feminine within the dreamer. Dreaming of a "real life" lover can suggest something in waking life that's unfolding in that relationship. However, the relationship can also be seen as one of the ways we are learning about ourselves and partners. Whether your dream lover is a symbolic construct, or a person in waking life, examining the characteristics reveals the dynamics of how our Psyche is connecting with these qualities and showing the issues underlying relationships. Remember to identify the three attributes that first come to mind for your dream lover. Are those qualities you admire, or behavior you want to change and improve?

Although not included in the eight main themes, dreams that include sex are not uncommon and can have levels and layers of meaning. Because of the many taboos, and highly-charged energy that surround the topic, it's important to examine the dream situation carefully. Dreaming of intimacy with a stranger, or someone you know who isn't your partner, is also not unusual. Think about the qualities and characteristics of that person, as the most common interpretation of these dreams is that person has something you want and would like to internalize. Or, in contrast, it could be a quality you don't want, especially if you are uncomfortable about the intimacy in the dream. Your own feelings about sexuality can also be a clue. Are you currently partnered and want to be in a more secure relationship? Do you long to feel desired? Most importantly, how do you feel about the dream? Does the dream situation feel "wrong" or natural in its own setting.

Clothing and Costumes

Clothes are said to represent our attitudes, how we "clothe" our opinions and views. When we look in the symbolic mirror of our dreams we view the current "costume" the dream portrays. If clothing seems to be an important symbol, notice the colors and styles—how are you attired? Clothes can indicate a readiness to face what's ahead or create a sense of being unprepared, which as noted elsewhere, is a common theme. You could find yourself in a Halloween costume in July or in a tattered shirt at the office before an important meeting. What is the condition of the clothing; are your garments clean and new, or old and worn?

Are you dressed appropriately for the situation or even the time period in history? You could be overdressed or underdressed, feeling either pleased and proud or ashamed. Are you changing clothes, which could indicate that a change of attitude is necessary? You may also be aware of a certain item of clothing and its purpose such as a hat (protect your head) or a belt (hold up your pants or skirt) or an apron (keep your clothes clean and protected).

Shoes can indicate the kind of activity and whether they are adequate and appropriate. Maybe you are running barefoot through summer grass, feeling wonderful, or trudging through pouring rain without boots or umbrella. The purpose of the clothing or accessory can be a clue to the message.

Places, Settings, and Scenes

The location and setting of dream scenes can reveal a great deal about the overall feeling and how you are processing waking life events. Are you walking along a sandy beach with waving palm trees, or lost and caught in rush hour traffic, trying to get somewhere in the middle of a big city? You might be struggling to walk through a blizzard or sitting in front of a cozy fire enjoying the snowfall outside.

Do you feel comfortable in the surroundings and "climate" of the dream, or is the location a place that has unhappy memories? Setting can also be related to weather, mentioned in the next chapter, as you could find yourself on a tropical island with a hurricane threatening from the horizon rather than blissfully basking on a sandy beach. Are you prepared to cope with the setting, or are you ill equipped to handle what the situation presents? Calm weather versus storms reveals the state of your emotions.

Time and Seasons

The time of day, or night, can indicate the stage of life or the phase of a current project. Do you feel that you have plenty of time in the dream, or are you rushing so you won't be late? The season of the year can also reflect the stage of life, or of a project, and also represent a time or holiday that you have strong feelings about. A setting of spring suggests new growth and potential, while autumn with falling leaves indicates that things are coming to the end of their cycle. Do you dream of a time of harvest or are you planting new seeds?

You might dream of a birthday party or walking in winter woods with gently falling snow. You might find yourself in a stark setting with bare trees that feels somewhat desolate. Take note if the dream is happening in present time or another era. You might dream of an event from your childhood or something in the ancient past or even the future. A past life dream might have a powerful message about karma and scores that need to be settled.

CHAPTER FIFTEEN

Dream Symbols:
Buildings, Vehicles, Travel, Weather

Sometimes a cigar is just a cigar.

~ Dr. Sigmund Freud, 1900

Buildings and Homes

One of the most common dream experiences is being inside a house or another kind of building. Descriptions may differ dramatically, and the house may not be where you live, but this image appears frequently. Because our state of mind is the central influence in the quality of our lives it's important to understand that symbolically "where we live" represents our consciousness and our prevailing state of mind. And in dreams, houses usually represent states of consciousness or awareness.

As with any other dream, the first things to be examined upon waking are thoughts, feelings, and emotions. Do you like the house and feel at home, or is the place unfamiliar with a sense of being lost and uncomfortable? Are you happy, sad, or frightened inside this structure? Paying attention to house metaphors over time will show how you live and move within your own consciousness. In this way the Soul's guidance is brought to self-conscious awareness, making an improvement in behavior and reversing self-defeating patterns.

As you work with the dream, consider the purpose of the building. Like clothes, the purpose and function of the structure are clues to decoding the symbols. Is the building a home, hospital, bank, or school? Maybe you're in a hotel, or even entering a church or temple. Are you in a simple one-level structure, or a high-rise apartment or condo? Maybe you're walking in a big mall in search of a department store. Is this a place you "own" or does it belong to someone else, and you are here temporarily, only passing through? What is the condition of the house or building? Is the building new or in need of repair with peeling paint and rotting wood?

When a house or building is the most prominent image, first identify where you are in relation to the house. Are you outside looking in, or inside feeling trapped, looking for a way out? In the first case it's a state of consciousness you're trying to achieve, or "get into." In the second case it's a mental state you're trying to change, shift, or transform from one state to another.

Do you know your way around, or do you wander lost and confused? Is the house new and empty, which indicates potential, or cluttered and filled with "dust collectors." These are metaphors for your waking state, revealing what needs to be recognized or changed. If the dream situation is pleasant, you're on the right track. If you are frightened and confused, then corrective action is necessary in waking life.

Dreaming of hotels or motels, which are temporary lodging and can be related to travel, usually represents direction. People often dream of being in large hotels with conference centers where they are attending lectures, or being a featured speaker, expected to "perform." Are you learning something new, or needing to deliver what is already known?

It's important to note who else is in your dream house. Who are the people and what rooms do they occupy? What are they doing? If this is "where you live" it's important to focus on the condition of consciousness being conveyed. Do you feel welcome, or like an unwelcome intruder?

People often dream of being in their parent's home or the place where they grew up. This usually suggests that the issue has its origin in the past. Perhaps it is a nagging and leftover incident from childhood that left a deep wound that needs to be healed. Without realizing this we draw similar circumstances to us, trying to get free of negative patterns.

If you are inside the house what level or floor are you on? The main level of the house represents waking self-consciousness in the same way that we spend most waking time on the "main floor." This is typically where we interact with other others if we have a family. This is usually where food is prepared and consumed, showing how we nurture ourselves. Is the house spacious, clean, and well-ordered, or do you find mess and clutter?

Basements or portions of the house that are underground, reveal what's going on beneath the surface. This can relate to material that is unconscious and is being presented symbolically by para-consciousness. Is the basement nicely finished and well lighted, or is it damp with cement blocks that are gray and dark? This reveals something about the underlying emotional basis of what's happening in day to day life. Garages are where vehicles are kept and are usually full of "stuff" that is often unused and forgotten. What symbolic boxes in storage need to be opened and sorted through? What needs to be donated to the Thrift Store, or even taken to the dump?

The upper level of a house symbolizes meta-consciousness or higher states of mind. If you are on an upper level, are you in an attic? Is it storming outside, indicating emotional turmoil? Does the roof leak? Is this room dark, dusty and full of old relics, or do you find yourself in a space where brilliant light from above is streaming into the room? With light shining through a higher window you are receiving guidance from your Higher Self. If the space is dark and foreboding, you are not listening.

Whether you are paying attention in waking life, can be gleaned from what you were doing on the main floor or in the basement. Transitions in house dreams are also important. Do you move between levels, showing progress forward with an issue, or do you get stuck somewhere in a dark room, indicating that your current mode of behavior in waking life is not constructive? Hallways are said to represent transitions or shifts in states of consciousness or awareness.

Cars, Trucks, and Other Vehicles

Certain aspects of dream symbolism seem to possess commonality for most dreamers. For example, as noted above, houses and buildings in dreams almost always reveal levels of consciousness, while cars and other vehicles reveal how we navigate the highway of life. Cars show how healthy or sturdy our "transportation" vehicle is and what may be needed for a particular circumstance. Cars/vehicles symbolize how easily we can move around and accomplish our work, and if on a road or highway, symbolize the direction we're headed, or trying to go.

When a vehicle appears in a dream, take note of the kind of vehicle and its purpose. Is it a sexy sports car built for pleasure and speed, and may be a major status symbol, or is it a big utility vehicle designed for hard work and heavy loads? Is the vehicle appropriate to the task at hand? Look at the setting in the dream to determine the nature of the work being done and what kind of material is being hauled—construction material or trash. Are you driving a "dump truck" or delivering critical supplies to a construction site? What needs to be off loaded in waking life, or what do you need for a new project? If the car is a convertible, that may indicate a desire for freedom with a sense of abandon with the wind in your hair. For another dreamer the fact that a "convertible" can change its form made indicate a need for flexibility.

What color is the vehicle and how do you feel about that color? A big red truck could signal too much aggression or hidden anger, while a peaceful blue or white color could be a more positive sign, indicating that you have (or need to find) more clarity. If the car is a luxury car, what might that say about your method of transport in waking life? A trendy sports car might indicate too much reliance on pure speed, or maybe even a tendency toward recklessness. In this case the message may be to slow down or be less concerned with outward appearances.

The most important thing to notice is whether you're in the driver's seat, meaning you're in charge of where you're headed. If you are a passenger trapped in the back seat, you may have no control over your direction, or feel out of control in waking life. Is the car moving, stopped, stuck in a ditch, or rushing out of control down a hill or embankment? If the vehicle isn't moving, but you're in the driver's seat, maybe it's time to step on the gas and make a change in life direction and move forward.

If you feel the vehicle is going too fast, and you can't control the speed or direction, then the message may be just the opposite. Slow down and take a hard look at your direction. Stop. Look. Listen. If you are in the back seat in your dream, feeling totally out of control about the direction, this probably means you need to take a more active role and make decisions that put you more in charge in waking life. You might need to stop letting someone else tell you what to do, and stop passively letting life happen.

Take note of the vehicle's operating condition. Do the headlights work, or are you driving in the dark? Is the accelerator stuck and you can't move forward, or are you out of control? Do you have enough fuel? What is the weather like? Is it a beautiful clear day, indicating maximum visibility that allows you to see where you're headed, or are you driving at night on a winding road in a rainstorm? What is the condition of the road? Are you on a well-maintained superhighway, or traveling along an isolated dirt road that is filled with holes? Are there obstacles in your path, or is the road ahead clear?

Where are you on the symbolic highway in your waking life? Are you excited about the situation or feeling frightened and overwhelmed? If you're behind the wheel of a sexy convertible, driving down a highway feeling good about life, that's probably a confirming message that all is well in terms of where you're headed and your ability to get there in style. Conversely, if you're driving a rickety old car, struggling to climb a hill with an accelerator that isn't working, then you need to take a hard look at the circumstances of your waking life and the condition of your physical "vehicle."

If you don't have enough "gas" or energy to accomplish what you need to do, you may be physically exhausted. A radical change of direction and a period of rest may be called for. You might also spend some time in your waking life visualizing your absolute "dream car." If money were no object, what car would you own? Reflect on what that vehicle says about your self-image and the direction of your dreams.

Travel: Planes, Trains, and Buses

Travel can reveal your literal direction in life, or your destiny. Travel is the current direction you're headed unless you change course. As mentioned in the vehicle section, the condition of the road offers clues to your current path. Are you at a crossroads where a course correction is called for, or does the way seem clear ahead? You could be stopped at a red light, or one that has just turned yellow, suggesting a warning to slow down.

Travel can also indicate a change of state, a break from routine, or a chance to rest and recharge. Sometimes travel can be work related, at other times travel could indicate family responsibility, such as a wedding or a funeral. Examining the departure location and the destination can reveal what is changing or what might need a new direction. Does the travel feel pleasant, or are you running to catch a train or plane and feeling stressed?

Travel dreams can also be connected to temporary lodging like hotels and motels. What feels temporary, or needs to be? It's important to notice who is traveling with you—happy companions or difficult people.

Trains move along a track that is attached to the ground and have a pre-determined destination and schedule. Are you rolling along on a hi-speed luxury train through beautiful landscapes, stuck in the station, or going through a dark tunnel? As a passenger on a train you are along for the ride and have no control over the destination, or where you arrive, unless you get off the train and choose another outcome.

Buses are similar to trains in symbolism as they have pre-determined routes and stops. If you are a passenger, you have no control, but if you are the driver, you have responsibility for the passengers. What is your role? Are you in a tour bus or a school bus? Does the bus break down, or are you relaxed and comfortable on a tour, enjoying the scenery and looking forward to your destination?

Airplanes fly high in the sky, partaking of the element of air. Planes are thought to suggest that we can view the matter from a higher level with a broader perspective than being on the ground. Planes get to their destination quicker than cars or trains. What does the craft look like? Is the plane a large commercial jet or a small plane? Are you the pilot, flying first class, or in the back of the plane in the crowded coach section? Is this a pleasure trip or related to work? Are the skies clear or stormy? Where might you need an objective aerial view in waking life?

Boats move on the element of water so the emotions are usually connected to this symbol. Are you cruising on a large ocean liner or paddling a row boat or canoe on a lake? Is the situation pleasant or uncomfortable? What is the condition of the water? Is the weather clear or stormy? Are things calm or dangerous? How are you navigating the waters of your emotions? Are you making good progress or bailing water to stay afloat?

Weather

As you journal your dream, describe the weather. Weather reveals your emotional "climate" and the state of your emotions in waking life. Since weather is constantly changing, this represents your shifting moods and responses. Weather is a common symbol and indicates the condition of your emotional nature and the potential for storms or smooth sailing in waking life. Is a storm brewing on the horizon, and do you have time to take cover, indicating there's time for a course correction in waking life?

Is the sun shining or is there lightning; does the sound of thunder excite or terrify you? Are you cozy and comfortable on a rainy day, or depressed, watching a bleak rainfall? Are you caught outside in a rain storm without an umbrella, or is it a warm summer rain and you want to joyfully splash and dance in a puddle? Are you trapped in a blinding blizzard, or having fun building a snow fort? Your response to the symbols and the circumstances in the dream are critical.

CHAPTER SIXTEEN

Dream Symbols:
Colors, Numbers, Gems and Crystals, Archetypes

One become two, two becomes three,
and out of the third comes the one as the fourth.

~ Maria Prophetissa, The Axiom of Alchemy

Color

Clinical research indicates that most dreams are in color, since that's how we see the daytime world, although noting whether a dream is in color or black and white can be significant. Researchers feel whether or not we remember the color in our dreams is an issue of recall more than symbolism. Some people claim that all their dreams are in color, and different hues and tones form an important part of their symbolic vocabulary, including everything from vibrant primaries to soft pastels.

People who dream in color are surprised and concerned when they have an occasional black and white dream. This could suggest that the issues being dealt with are fairly clear cut or are shown in stark contrast. Other dreamers recall only black and white images where color is not part of the landscape. In some dreams no color might mean that passion is lacking, or the dreamer is disconnected from feelings, as intense colors usually indicate strong feelings and vitality.

Complete color blindness is rare, and people who were not born color blind, or color weak, can still dream in color since their brain remembers. A full color dream that shows up for someone who usually remembers their dreams in monochrome can be a startling experience that gets noticed and remembered.

The significance of color equates to a spectrum of expression, like the colors of the rainbow. Gold and silver are colors but also metals that have intrinsic value and can be made into jewelry and other artifacts. Color may be an overall sense or tone, or one image can stand out dramatically like a tall man in a bright green cloak or a little girl wearing a yellow scarf. Notice how you feel about a particular color and whether the colors are muted or washed out or painted in vibrant hues with lots of light.

A rainbow is formed when white light, containing all the colors of the visible spectrum, is refracted through a lens. So, the presence or absence of color is intrinsically connected to the corresponding amount of light and may carry this message in dreams. To analyze secondary colors, like yellow-green or red-violet, which combine two primaries, look at the meaning of the primary colors listed below. Secondary colors that stand out in dreams can sometimes indicate transitions, moving from one state to another.

Is the significant color in your dream one you like or dislike? This speaks to opening to the influence or integrating what that color represents or vibrates in your energy field. What follows are brief suggested meanings for the seven colors of the rainbow, black, white, gray, and brown. These are just suggestions and idea starters.

✧　✧　✧

Red: The color of blood, battle, and the life force. Red is a vital color that is full of energy. "Seeing red," or waving a red flag in front of a bull, can indicate unexpressed anger that is potentially dangerous. "In the red" means financial difficulty and could be a warning to curb spending. Red can indicate the need to stop (like a traffic light) and slow your pace in waking life. Are you expressing too much energy or not enough? How are you directing your energy? Is anger an issue at present?

Orange: The color of the Sun, and reminiscent of colorful autumn leaves, orange is warming and stimulating to the circulatory system. Orange is an empowering energy that is usually seen as positive. Orange in a dream can indicate that a surplus of energy and "fuel" is available or needs to be directed in a more positive manner. Orange is a color of fall and also connected to the holiday of Halloween. This could indicate a timing issue.

Yellow: The color of the mind and mental energy. In some settings yellow implies cowardice as in the expression a "yellow streak." Where are your thoughts and mental patterns holding you back? Are you frightened about something in waking life? What new thoughts or mental patterns need to be developed in order to move ahead? Are you thinking too much? Perhaps you need to consider some bright new ideas.

Green: Ordinarily suggests new growth and healing, but the shade of green is important to note as certain shades could indicate illness. Are you "green with envy," or looking for "green energy," meaning money? Is it a drab color you wouldn't think of wearing, or something bright and cheerful that feels uplifting, like the feeling of spring or a fresh new start?

Blue: A cool color, sometimes meaning "feeling blue," or sad. Blue is also a healing color and is used on some hospital walls to reduce inflammation and slow heart rate. Blue can indicate a need to calm down and temper strong emotions and not use force of will. Does the blue appear in the sky or in the waters of a lake or ocean? What are your feelings?

Indigo: Indigo is a blend of blue and violet and is one of the rainbow colors although a secondary, a combination of two colors. Indigo is grounding and anchoring to mental processes and is seen as a spiritual color. Indigo is thought to be a color or frequency that creates a bridge to higher realms. Indigo in a dream could indicate strong guidance.

Purple/Violet: The color of royalty, nobility, and ritual. Purple often implies wisdom and enhanced status as well as having a spiritual significance. Purple is also a color associated with ceremony, magic, and a sense of the sacred, relating to priests and priestesses. Purple and violet can also represent wealth and luxury.

Black: Black pigment contains all the shades of color, and like a womb, holds potential; a black night cloaks and hides the colors of day, carrying the idea of concealment. Darkness, or a sense of blackness, generally indicates that you're feeling in the "dark," and can't see a way out. Black also indicates what is hidden or concealed or is like a container of potential. Do things get darker or lighter as the dream progresses? Does the darkness feel threatening or is it protecting you from a threat? Does the darkness conceal something not yet ready to be seen? We can only see the stars on a dark night, and this could indicate guidance. Do you feel frightened, curious, or safe?

White: White light contains all the colors of the visible spectrum, and a white paper connotes potential, the idea of *carte blanche.* In contrast to black, white implies light, and the ability to see, suggesting clarity, guidance, illumination, and sometimes purity. The idea of white and light can cast things in sharp contrast that can't be ignored. Secrets and mysteries are revealed in the white light of understanding. However, light can be so bright we can't open our eyes to see what's there. We can't look directly at the Sun.

Gray: A neutral balance of all the colors that on the higher side can imply spiritual mastery, especially where clothing is concerned, like the gray cloak of the Hermit in Tarot. Depending on the context gray can also symbolize depression or listlessness. Gray can represent dark clouds that hide the light of the Sun or a lack of energy. Gray can also suggest that things are not clear, and it's not yet time to make a decision. Perhaps gray is counseling the need for neutrality in a situation.

Brown: The color of earth can indicate either a sense of dullness or something that is ready to be plowed and tended. Is the shade of brown like rich loamy soil, ready to be planted, or damp mud that is difficult to get through? Brown can mean being, or needing to be, grounded and practical, or a need to be "down to earth." Brown can indicate a vast field of potential new growth or a sense of being stuck in something that is muddy and unclear.

Numbers

Numbers have practical significance in life for accounting and tracking, but they also have symbolical significance. To the Pythagoreans numbers were seen as divine energy. Numbers can appear in dreams as dates, months, seasons, phone numbers, and room numbers. The number might show up as a quantity of objects or people, or the number might repeat in the dream, highlighting the importance of the symbol. Numbers appearing together can show how to combine their separate meanings. Numbers can indicate timing. Sometimes a number on a sign can be a timing clue that relates to a date, or the number of days, weeks, or months that will elapse before the issue is resolved. Do you see it on a door as a room number, indicating a state of consciousness, something to be entered into when you cross the threshold? Maybe you hold a winning lottery ticket in the dream and the message is to buy a ticket, or invest in something in waking life.

✿   ✿   ✿

0. Potential: Zero is literally "no thing" and represents the unlimited potential of a circle or a state of void before a cycle of manifestation. The symbol for zero is usually represented as an oval like an egg, but it is actually symbolically an infinite circle before the dot at the center focuses a point of creative expression. In dreams zero's symbolism is either subtle or dramatic, often signaling a huge change or period of uncertainty about what happens next. Perhaps it's time to take a leap?

1. Initiation: One is always first and stands alone. Symbolically one cannot be divided. Meanings of the number 1 include initiation, unity, beginning, initiative, singleness, isolation, originality, and self-consciousness. The vertical, linear form of the Arabic numeral 1 shows initiation of movement and begins with the vertical line that connects above to below. The concept of 1 can also be represented by a dot, sometimes shown at the center of a circle, which is the astrological symbol of the Sun. When the number 1 is a key symbol in a dream, look for what stands alone or what may need to be viewed in isolation. Where are opportunities for new beginnings, originality, or a need to stand on your own. What needs to happen first?

2. *Duplication:* 2 is seen symbolically as a line that connects two dots, or as the Roman numeral II, the perfect doubling of 1. 2 is a mirror image, created by addition, and is the first divisible number. Meanings of the number 2 include duplication, duality, reflection, replication, division, recreation, receptivity, dependence, polarity, opposition, division, double, twin, mirror image, antagonism, opposite or complementary energies. 2 can be either divided or multiplied. When the number 2 manifests as a symbol in a dream look for issues of duality, relationship, partnership, or mirroring. What needs to be duplicated or replicated? What is the core issue teaching by reflection or relationship? What do you need to look at? What is the "magic mirror" trying to reveal? Facing your true reflection requires courage.

3. *Multiplication:* 3 expresses the perfect outworking of the principles of 1 and 2, increasing through multiplication, and is geometrically depicted as a triangle. Meanings include multiplication, trinity, development, imagination, growth, creativity, unfoldment, procreation, and expression. When threes appear as dream symbols look for what needs to grow or what may be multiplying without your conscious awareness. Is the growth constructive, or happening like weeds choking your garden? When threes appear in dreams look for clues where growth may be blocked or needs to occur.

4. *Stability:* 4 is shown as a square. The expression four-square suggests stability and solidity. Meanings of the number 4 include classification, order, reason, measurement, recording, planning, surveying, naming, tabulating, stability, geometry, and topography. Fours appearing in dreams may reveal where the situation is either stable and grounded, or stagnant, showing what needs to move and become unblocked. Fours may also indicate where the situation requires grounding and needs to become more stable.

5. *Change:* 5 stands in the middle of the numbers 1 – 9 and is an ancient symbol of humanity since a human figure with arms outstretched and legs spread wide resembles a pentagram, a five-pointed star, like Leonardo da Vinci's Vitruvian Man. Meanings of the number 5 include mediation, change, adaptation, means, agency, activity, process, uncertainty, instability, transition, and versatility. Fives as dream symbols may show where change is occurring below the surface of self-conscious awareness. Fives in dreams may further reveal where change is needed but being resisted. Where do you need to adapt? Are things in motion and shifting, or do they need to be?

6. *Balance:* 6 shows balance and symmetry, sometimes depicted as two intersecting triangles that represent the union of opposites. Meanings of the number 6 include equilibration, harmony of opposites, balanced polarities, reciprocity, love, and complementary activities. Sixes in dreams may indicate the reciprocal nature of the energy required in a situation—balancing and harmonizing opposite polarities. Sixes may reveal where relationship requires balance or what quality is needed to bring about equilibrium and harmony. What is out of balance in waking life?

7. *Victory:* The ancient word for the number 7 meant "oath" and implied the fulfillment of a sworn compact. Meanings of the number 7 include temporary cessation, rest, safety, security, peace, health, wealth and satisfaction, recognition and spiritual forces. Sevens in dreams may hint at the awakening and movement of spiritual awareness in the dreamer's life and may reveal the path ahead after a period without forward progress. Sevens in dreams may cast additional light on the nature of the spiritual quest and provide guidance during a difficult period of transition. Sevens appear in many systems, including "on the seventh day God rested." 7 is like a plateau, taking stock, before the final ascent. A rest or retreat may be in order.

8. *Rhythm:* 8 implies the ebb and flow, flux and reflux, of a single breath-like motion--like ocean tides. The figure 8 viewed horizontally is the symbol of infinity, implying a continual back and forth movement of energy. Meanings of the number 8 include vibration, rhythm, involution and evolution, and resurrection. After pausing to rest in 7, energy moves and flows again in 8. In dreams, eights may offer insight into where a compensating balance of energy might be found to harmonize the flow. Eights in dreams can also indicate the manner in which the dreamer needs to restore rhythm and a sense of give and take.

9. *Completion:* 9 embodies the pure, clear expression of the idea or impulse that began in 1 and completes a cycle. Meanings of the number 9 include completion, culmination, attainment, fulfillment, goal of endeavor, termination, and the end of a cycle. Nines in dreams almost always reveal what is concluding and what is now passing. Nines can shed light on how release can be achieved more easily, usually pointing toward a profound moment of release and letting go.

10. *Dominion:* The number 10 combines the 1 of new beginnings with the 0 of potentiality, starting a new cycle at a higher level of expression. Meanings of the number 10 include dominion, perfection, mastery, embodiment, consummation, order of magnitude, a grand finale and a return to unity. There is a sense of mastering one phase and preparing for a new level—like a graduation. Tens in dreams indicate both what needs to pass away as well as the new cycle that begins at a new level of expression. Tens in dreams may reveal the area of life to look ahead for the next chapter, showing where to build and what to leave behind.

❁ ❁ ❁

In basic numerology the objective is to arrive at a number between 1 and 10 by reduction. Reducing numbers by adding them together, and then reducing the total, arriving at the smallest single number from 1-10. For example, 322 is 3 + 2 + 2 = 7. Likewise, 1001 is 1 + 1 = 2. 978 is 9 + 7 + 8 = 24, so add 2 + 4 = 6 to get the lowest single digit number.

11, 22, and 33: These are often called master numbers. In most systems of numerology these numbers are not reduced; otherwise 11 would reduce to 2 and 22 would reduce to 4 and 33 to 6. These numbers are said to strain the nervous system in numerology charts.

11 seems to be similar in nature to the planet Uranus in that it operates on a mental plane at a higher frequency. It is difficult to contain and can be a disruptive influence but the energy is transformative. In dreams this may signal the need to look for solutions that are out of the ordinary.

22 seems to hold new patterns of manifestation and has been called the Master Builder. There are 22 letters in the Hebrew alphabet and 22 cards in the Major Arcana of Tarot. 22 in a dream might be an indication to open to spiritual counsel and be prepared for a totally new and supercharged way of orienting to life.

33 is said to carry the most spiritual potential. 33 is sometimes called the "Master Teacher." Because 33 is the sum of 11 and 22 it carries a powerful meaning.

Crystals, Gems and Jewels

If a stone or gem appears in your dream, notice if it's in a natural state, rough and unpolished, or still in the Earth. Stones and uncut minerals represent things in potential. If a crystal or gem has been mined, cleaned, and polished this may reveal its inner worth or value as a cut and polished jewel. The stone or gem could be a treasure or seem like a worthless piece of rock from a monetary standpoint. Something may be "crystal clear" or a "diamond in the rough."

If the stone has been incorporated into a piece of jewelry, that changes the significance from a purely symbolic or vibratory meaning to something that has been altered by human intervention. Jewelry has been fashioned by human hands in addition to the forces of nature, and like art, adds perceived value based on its outer presentation. A piece of jewelry can be a gift, a reward, a treasure, a talisman, or a stone of power.

Certain stones are believed to have great power. Some have been used for healing and others have been valued for other attributes. Perhaps the stone that appears in your dream has been incorporated into an amulet or talisman, suggesting even more power or meaning in a ritual. What would this mean if you could hold it in your hand in waking consciousness?

I once had a dream where I was told I could choose a gift of any pair of coral earrings from a case of jewelry. Coral comes from the sea, so I believed at the time that the message was to pay close attention to my feelings as I was going through a difficult time. Was the emotional tide coming in or going out? Soon after I found a pair of silver earrings, surrounding coral spheres, that I could wear as a potent reminder of the dream's message.

Crystals grow in accordance with mathematical structure, according to principles of what is sometimes called sacred geometry. The external geometric form of a crystal is the outward, visible expression of the mineral's internal atomic structure. This matrix is at the heart of any crystal and also determines characteristics such as hardness, fracture, and cleavage and its relation to every specimen of the same mineral. Because crystals hold a numeric frequency of shape and form they also have a relationship to the significance of that number.

Depending on the source, there are six or seven basic crystal systems that include the familiar six-sided quartz crystal and the pyramidal nature of fluorite crystals. Some have exotic names like orthorhombic and triclinic. Several of these relate to what are known as the five

Platonic solids: cube, dodecahedron, icosahedron, octahedron, and tetrahedron, which is the nature of fluorite. Any time shapes are a key element in dream symbolism, this adds the meaning of number to the equation. Another aspect to notice is the color of the stone and how that combines with the geometry.

Minerals are formed in nature by one of two forces--fire or water--that are also the two main archetypal elements. Minerals formed by fire are called igneous and those formed by the slow action of water are called sedimentary. A third classification is really a combination of the two. These are called metamorphic. At a subtle level the kind of stone says something about what's forming in your life. Are you working with the fire of passion or the flow of emotions? What metamorphosis needs to occur, or what has been slowly building up or wearing away over time?

If a stone, mineral, or gem appears in your dreams, always examine your feelings. Does the object belong to you as a treasure, or is it something you desire, or even covet? In what period of history or prehistory does the dream sequence occur? This can provide a big clue to the deeper meaning of the symbol. According to the American psychic, Edgar Cayce, a giant quartz crystal, called the Tuoai Stone, was the central power-generating force of ancient Atlantis, and the eventual cause of the island nation's demise.

https://beadage.net/gemstones/

Meanings of some stones and crystals are listed below.

Amber: Constancy

Amethyst: Clarity

Beryl: Courage

Carnelian: Warmth

Clear quartz: Purity and communication

Diamond: Abundance

Garnet: Devotion

Emerald: Truth

Jade: The Soul

Lapis: Creativity, and soothing

Malachite: Balance

Moonstone: Grace

Opal: Gift of prophecy

Pearls: The deep memory of the sea

Peridot: Wisdom

Rose quartz: Opens the heart

Ruby: Passion

Sapphire: Insight

Onyx: Grounding and spiritual strength

Topaz: Faithfulness

Tourmaline: Deeply calming

Archetypes

The word archetype comes from the Greek word *arketypon*, which means "something molded first as a model." Major archetypal figures appear in stories and movies. The familiar archetypal characters are: Hero, Mentor, Ally, Herald, Trickster, Guardian, and Shadow/Villain. These roles, most of which are cast in movies, round out the story and move the plot along. Each archetypal character provides a particular quality as he or she interacts with the "hero," the main character. In the same way, archetypal symbols may appear in our dream stories with a message about what role we might be playing in life.

Carl Jung and Joseph Campbell both worked with the idea of archetypes. Jung was very interested in astrology, and according to some sources, he used the planets, which were gods to the ancients who embodied certain qualities and characteristics, as his basic meaning structure as he was developing his theory of archetypes. In the work of both Campbell and Jung, there are most commonly twelve major archetypes: Jester/Fool, Innocent, Magician (wizard), Lover, Ruler/Monarch, Sage/Wise one, Hero, Explorer, Creator/Artist, Caregiver, Rebel/Outlaw, and Everyman. Many researchers have attempted to draw parallels between these and the zodiac signs, although the correspondences are not totally equivalent.

Psychologist Carol S. Pearson, PhD, in her book, *Awakening the Heroes Within: Twelve Archetypes to Help us find Ourselves and Transform our World*, also describes twelve archetypes. Building on the earlier work of Jung and Campbell, Pearson uses the categories of Innocent, Orphan, Warrior, Caregiver, Seeker (wanderer), Lover, Destroyer, Creator, Ruler (monarch), Magician, Sage and Fool.

Zodiac Signs

Another example of collective, cultural, and personal symbols and archetypes are the signs of the zodiac. Each zodiac sign represents one or more essential qualities. Regardless of our open-mindedness and self-perceived objectivity, we all have biases about Zodiac signs. Where our own sign is concerned we may have strong feelings about how to do it "right" and be tempted to judge others for what we perceive as not measuring up. As a result, if a Zodiac sign shows up in a dream, feelings and strong opinions about that sign will color and shape what the dream symbol is trying to convey. Do you need to incorporate these symbolic energies in your own nature or should you modify your beliefs and actions toward others?

As a way to further illustrate the point, what follows is a positive characteristic of each zodiac sign paired with a more judgment-laden or negative stereotype of the same quality. If we're honest, we all fall prey to stereotyping or turning others into caricatures of archetypal energy. Observe your own opinions or feelings. Dream symbols give clues to our true feelings if we open our minds to listen.

Zodiac Sign	Positive Quality	Negative Stereotype
Aries	active	rash
Taurus	determined	bull-headed
Gemini	curious	nosey
Cancer	sensitive	moody
Leo	confident	arrogant
Virgo	discerning	critical
Libra	balanced	indecisive
Scorpio	astute	secretive
Sagittarius	generous	spend thrift
Capricorn	ambitious	power hungry
Aquarius	independent	aloof
Pisces	empathetic	detached

How objective was your response? You might create an astrology category in your *Dream Diary*, which will grow as you identify your own response and biases. Then watch for these Sun Sign characters to appear in your dreams.

CHAPTER SEVENTEEN

Dream Symbols:
Animals, Birds, Aquatic Creatures, Insects

I want to be like a caterpillar:
eat a lot, sleep for a while, wake up beautiful.

~ Anonymous

Animals

Animals are common dream symbols and are said to represent instinctual qualities. We have much to learn from our animal friends and fellow creatures. Meaning can relate to your feelings about the animal and whether the animal seems friendly or threatening. It's important to identify the animal in detail: size, color, posture, or actions. Are you excited to encounter this creature, curious, or terrified? Is the animal wild or tame, a beloved pet, or a stray, looking for a home?

The animal in your dream may be saying that you can already draw on its qualities in waking life, or you may feel frightened because you don't yet know how to exhibit this particular characteristic. As mentioned in the list below, bear symbolizes strength and power across most traditions, but in a dream that strength could cause fear if the bear is attacking. Instead you might dream of a mother bear with her cubs. Do you dream of a bear because you need strength in your life, or do you feel overpowered by a dominating figure in your life and desire to run? The bear in a dream may counsel to face your fear.

Some examples of animal symbolism include bulls, which symbolize strength, prowess, and stubbornness. Cows and other cattle have symbolized nurturing, wealth, and domestic urges for ages. Cats embody curiosity and resilience as in the fabled "nine lives." Felines are nocturnal hunters, showing their skill at finding things in the dark. Cats also have an Egyptian connection and convey both independence and mystery. Do you dream of a playful kitten or a panther on the prowl? Do you feel affection or fear?

Horses are generally seen to represent the human body and the ability to move through space since horses were our earlier vehicles. Many myths link horses to the Sun and convey magical rides through the sky like the famous winged steed, Pegasus. By contrast, the humble mouse may indicate what's hidden from every day awareness, concealed in a dark corner, and perhaps indicate where you are being opportunistic in nature. Maybe you need to operate behind the scenes, or instead, come out into the open.

Dragons are mythical beings that usually symbolize transformation and the alchemical process of the Great Work. As noted in a previous chapter, "dragon" comes from the Greek *drakon*, which means "watcher." And it's also worth noting again that dragons are said to hoard gold, which is a symbol of wisdom and mastery in alchemy. They are seen as threshold guardians, protecting hidden treasure and secret knowledge. Dragons are sometimes seen as positive, and at other times seen as miserly. In Chinese tradition members of the royal family are believed to be descendants of white dragons who were very wise and beneficent beings who came from the stars.

Serpents are also complex symbols that represent wisdom in many traditions, while in other cases can represent temptation and sexual energy. Snakes slithering on the ground may have a different meaning and arouse fear, while a cobra with its hood spread may inspire a sense of awe, representing the rising of the *kundalini* fire along the spine and the ruling power of a pharaoh. Once again, examine the context and your feelings. Ted Andrews book, *Animal Speak: The Spiritual &*

Magical Powers of Creature's Great & Small, is a great resource. What follows are the meanings of a few common animals.

Bat: Guardian of the night; rebirth; clairaudience

Bear: Strength, motherhood

Cat: Curiosity, mystery, magic

Coyote: Trickster, humor, hidden wisdom

Deer: Gentleness, mindfulness, regeneration

Dog: Loyalty, devotion, protection

Fox: Cunning, cleverness, playfulness

Horse: Freedom, power, movement

Lion: Courage, gold, Sun

Rabbit: Fertility, abundance, fear

Racoon: Mask, resourcefulness, scavenger

Seal: Playful, swim with the current

Squirrel: Resourceful, hoarding, spirited

Turtle: Longevity, endurance, innocence

Birds

Birds are typically universal symbols of messages from the spirit world, although depending on the dream "story," can also represent leaving the nest or feathering the nest. Birds lay eggs to give birth, so can represent potential that needs to be nurtured. The capacity for flight makes birds natural couriers from the human realm to higher planes. Birds denote flight, freedom, an aerial view, and an opening to the higher self. Crows usually represent news, although traditions vary whether the crow brings good news or is a harbinger of ill fortune. The owl, a nocturnal hunter, can be a symbol of wisdom or death, depending on the tradition.

A white dove is generally a symbol of peace and also signifies the soul. White doves are sacred to Venus, and are also symbols of the Holy Spirit and the Great Mother. Ducks appear to glide effortlessly on the surface of water, but underneath they are paddling like mad. Look for a play on words, for example, are you "ducking" an issue? Geese were sacred birds in ancient temples and acted as fierce protectors. Geese are highly territorial and may signal that you are being over-protective or that you need to guard something. And whimsically, you may be ready to "lay a golden egg," producing something of great value.

The eagle is a high soaring bird who sees clear and far. Mythology says the eagle is the only bird unafraid to fly in a storm and is the first to see the rising sun. Magpies are birds of great power to Indian tribes, but can often equate to a noisy nuisance to others. The Robin is seen as the harbinger of spring in certain locations and usually carries a positive connotation.

A swan is a symbol of the soul in many cultures, and the haunting sound of a dying swan, known as a "swan song" is a phrase that implies an ending. By contrast, hummingbirds are icons of joy and strength out of all proportion to their tiny size. Vultures, like scorpions, are known to be good mothers, fiercely protective of their young. Because they eat carrion, vultures, like the Egyptian god Anubis, are symbols of transformation. The vulture goddess Nekhbet was the ancient symbol of Upper Egypt, which was in the south where the Nile river originated. In Indian tradition woodpeckers are drummers and herald messages and perhaps indicate new rhythms in your life. Even though they make a lot of noise, they are the shiest of birds.

If a bird appears in your dream, consider if the bird is caged, in flight, or perched and watching you. What kind of bird is it; a high-flying raptor, a shy forest bird, or a water bird? Each has a unique quality and their element can reveal what level of mind or emotions you are dreaming about. Most importantly, what are your feelings about the bird both in the dream and upon waking?

What follows are some traditional meanings of certain birds. This link has more: *https://www.worldbirds.org/bird-symbolism/*

Blue bird: Happiness

Blue jay: Protection

Condor: Strength

Crane: Good fortune

Cuckoo: Timing

Dove: Peace

Eagle: Courage

Falcon: Victory

Flamingo: Generosity

Goose: Bravery

Hawk : Power

Hummingbird: Joy

Magpie: Intelligence

Owl: Wisdom (or ill omen)

Parrot: Patience

Peacock: Nobility

Phoenix: Transformation

Raven: Messenger

Stork: Birth

Swallow: Cheer

Swan : Love

Woodpecker: Signals

Aquatic animals

Dolphins are seen as magical guides to the spirit world and have been known to rescue humans in danger. They are mammals who partake of the elements of water and air and also have language. Their appearance in a dream may signal a message that needs to be heard or decoded. Whales are thought to represent memory and the deep and ancient knowing that comes from the ocean.

Fish are considered to be messengers that arise from the para-conscious level. In Japan, carp, or *Koi* fish, are a symbol of strength since they are the only fish that can conquer the waterfalls of the Yellow River. In China the scales and whiskers of *Koi* are thought to resemble those of a dragon and are therefore seen as a powerful and positive symbol.

What kind of fish appears in your dream and what are the color(s)? Are the fish in a river, ocean, or an aquarium? Are you swimming with sharks, and in danger, or snorkeling in a clear pool with small brightly colored fish? Is the water clear or cloudy? Always examine the surrounding situation and your feelings.

Insects

Insects have six legs, and sometimes wings, while other creatures like spiders and scorpions have eight legs and can be poisonous. Butterflies, bees, and lady bugs usually have a positive connotation while flies, mosquitoes, and wasps are typically considered to be pests. Flies in a dream may suggest something that is "bugging" you in waking life. Ants, like bees, are industrious creatures. Bees produce honey, but they can also sting, and most people would not be happy about a large ant hill appearing in their front yard. You might encounter an unusual hummingbird moth or a caterpillar. If insects appear in a dream look for what is happening and how it makes you feel. Cockroaches crawling in the darkness of a kitchen cabinet creates a very different feeling than beautiful butterflies in a sunny meadow.

CHAPTER EIGHTEEN

Dream Symbols:
Food, Flowers, Plants and Trees

*Pay attention to your dreams — God's angels
often speak directly to our hearts when we are asleep."*

~ Eileen Elias Freeman, *The Angels' Little Instruction Book, 1994*

Food

Food is perhaps the most basic human need; without food and water we would not survive. Dreams where food is a predominant symbol likely symbolize how we are "getting fed," or being nurtured. Or, do we go hungry? The meaning of food in dreams can range from a warning about diet and health to a deeper symbolism of what we really need. In my own dream that I called *Messenger Bag*, I was not getting fed or nurtured, and I set off to find something more satisfying. In that dream my search for food symbolized my work and the need to honor my calling.

Not only is the type of food important but also the setting and circumstances. Are you sitting down to a Thanksgiving banquet with loved ones and feeling happy, or are you hungry, feeling desperate, and in search of a meal? You might be offered a food item you dislike or looks toxic and you are resisting; this could be a message about something you need to "take in" and absorb in waking life. Or the message could be something your "taking" in waking life that you need to stop. Are you offered a plain lettuce salad or a rich dessert? Like other dream symbols, the colors, surroundings, and the appeal of the food are all important to examine.

Flowers

Each spring as sap runs through the trees again and seasonal birds return, stirring our hearts with their songs, we eagerly anticipate spring flowers. Hearty bulbs poke green shoots through thawing ground, and soon golden crocus, purple iris, yellow daffodils, and red tulips return color to the stark landscape of winter. We know that color has meaning, but what about the nature and quality of flowers and plants themselves?

The idea of "saying it with flowers" began long before the modern icon of FTD floral delivery. The language and symbolism of flowers, herbs, and plants has a rich history. In Constantinople in the 1600s, which later became Istanbul, flowers grew to have meaning and actually became a sophisticated code, enabling lovers and others to send symbolic messages. Each flower in a bouquet had a meaning. The language of flowers was introduced to Europe by Lady Mary Wortley Montagu, a society poet of the day, and a celebrated letter writer. In 1716 she accompanied her husband to the Turkish court in Istanbul. As a result of her discovery of the language of flowers she brought the code back to England where it found fertile soil.

After coming to England, the idea passed to the French, and subsequently back to England during Victoria's reign through Madame de la Tour's book *Le Langage des Fleurs*. The lusty French version proved too risqué for refined English society, and subsequent versions had to be toned down. One wonders what spicy sentiments might have been lost.

More than 800 flowers came to have distinct meaning in the floral code, and the messages encoded in bouquets could be both subtle and complex. Author David Squire gives an example, "Gillyflower and heliotrope with a leaf of Virginia creeper would mean "I offer true friendship, affection, and devotion." While another bouquet of monkshood, mountain ash, and blue violet conveys, "Danger is near; be prudent and faithful."

Flowers embody beauty and the ephemeral nature of life in form. They are the reproductive organs of plants, inviting bees and humming birds through their colors and scents, who in turn affect pollination. They also represent the eventual blooming and fruition of the Soul. Is the flower a bud, just opening its heart to the Sun, or a fading blossom? This may indicate the stage of the subject matter: beginning, maturing, or winding down.

What kind of flower appears? What color? How many petals, which might combine a message of number? Is it a wildflower in a native setting, or a cultivated hot house bloom? Are you picking the flower yourself? Is it a State flower? Is the aroma pleasing? Do you receive the flower(s) as a gift, and does this flower have a special meaning to you? Always examine your feelings as that's where the power lies.

What follows is a small selection of a few flowers and their meanings. This is just a sampling, and these meanings may differ for you as para-consciousness may have formed associations that relate to the season of the year or past events. Even so, their significance resides in the collective unconscious and may therefore now appear in a dream. The link is to a longer list of flower meanings.

https://en.wikipedia.org/wiki/Plant_symbolism

> Amaryllis: Pride
> Cherry blossom: Kindness and gentleness
> Chrysanthemum: Cheerfulness
> Clover: Industry
> Columbine: Resolution
> Daffodil: New beginnings and regard
> Daisy: Innocence
> Dandelion: Love's oracle
> Iris: Purple iris is wisdom and hope of spring
> Jasmine: Wealth
> Lavender: Relaxation

Lilac: White, youthful innocence; Purple, first love

Lily: White, purity and wisdom; Yellow, majesty

Lily of the Valley: Happiness

Lotus: Rebirth and the unfoldment of the Soul

Marigold: Grief

Orchid: Refined beauty

Pansy: Thoughts of others

Poinsettia: Mirth and celebration

Poppy: Red poppy, sacrifice and remembrance

Rose: Bud, youth; Red, desire and true love;
        White, innocence and purity; Pink, grace

Sunflower: Optimism and confidence

Tulip: Unconditional love

Violets: Faithfulness

Plants and Herbs

Plants and crops represent growth, potentially nurturing food, cultivation, and healing herbs. Are the plants in your dream well rooted and thriving, or are they withering from lack of water and care? What is the stage of growth? Are the plants wild in a field, growing in careful rows on a farm, or house plants that are lovingly cared for in a sunny window. Do you dream of weeds that are choking healthy plants? Poisonous plants could be a warning about toxic people in your life. Do you see a field of golden wheat or a parched area of dying crops?

The short list below notes only a few plant symbols. The link has more: *https://www.proflowers.com/blog/plant-symbolism-guide*

Plants

Aloe: Healing

Bamboo: Good fortune and longevity

Barley: Fertility

Bonsai: Balance and calm

Cactus: Protection and endurance

Cabbage: Profit

Corn: Fertility and abundance

Fichus: Abundance and peace

Ivy: Endurance and faithfulness

Money Tree: Wealth

Oats: Kindness and nutrition

Pomegranate: Regeneration

Shamrock: Good luck

Snake plant: Cleanliness

Spider plant: Mindfulness

Succulents: Loyalty

Wheat: Resurrection

Wisteria: Romance

Herbs

Basil: Success

Bay laurel wreath: Glory

Fennel: Strength

Garlic: Omen of magic

Ginger: Enthusiasm

Rosemary: Fidelity

Sage: Wisdom and respect

Thyme: Courage

Turmeric: Purifying

Yarrow: Healing

Trees

Because of their perennial beauty, gifts, and many uses trees are important symbols in diverse cultures. The idea of a Tree of Life appears in almost every culture, and mythically, the Tree of Life often grows in a magical garden, usually presided over by a goddess. The Tree is protected by some mythical creature, usually a wise guardian serpent or dragon, and bears a fruit, generally apples, which bestow immortality. In Chinese mythology the Tree of Life bears peaches.

In the Garden of Eden in the book of Genesis there were two notable trees; the Tree of the Knowledge of Good and Evil, which got Eve into so much trouble, and the Tree of Life. Unlike the Biblical story, the earlier Mesopotamian version of the tale casts the serpent in a positive role as a beneficent revealer of wisdom. Serpents are often seen as symbols of wisdom as noted in the animal section.

When trees appear as a central or significant dream symbol there can be multiple layers of meaning. Deciduous trees have an annual cycle that could imply a timing message, so examine the season of the year in which the tree appears. The tree may have green leaves in winter, or is barren in summer, both of which give clues to the waking life situation, showing that something is out of phase. Even evergreen trees drop their cones in an annual cycle. Does the tree have new spring buds, green leaves, glorious autumn foliage, or bare branches?

Perhaps the tree in your dream is a fruit tree. Is the tree in flower or heavily laden with ripe fruit or nuts that are ready to drop? Is the tree healthy? Where is the tree growing? In a garden? In a field? Is the tree covered with lights and holiday decorations, or a palm tree, swaying gently by an ocean?

The ancient Celts had a zodiac of trees where thirteen trees corresponded with the seasons and have qualities similar to the zodiac signs. (Helena Paterson, *The Celtic Lunar Zodiac*) *https://www. amazon.com/Celtic-Lunar-Zodiac-Interpret-Your/dp/156718510X*

Beginning with spring equinox the trees move around the seasonal wheel: Alder, Willow, Hawthorn, Oak, Holly, Hazel, Vine, Ivy, Reed, Elder, Birch, Rowan, and Ash. If one of these thirteen trees appear in a dream, the meaning could be even deeper link to your ancient past.

Are there several trees, each standing out in its own way? Is the tree part of a dense forest or standing alone like a sentinel? Are you walking in twisted brambles in a thicket or standing beneath a towering ancient oak? Is the tree about to be cut down for its wood? Is there a sense of protection as you stand beneath the branches, or is the scene stormy where the tree is struck by lightning, conveying an image like the Tower in Tarot? What part of the tree is most noticeable: the trunk that supports the structure, the roots that feed the tree and ground it in the earth, or the branches that reach to the sky?

If a tree appears in your dream, be grateful for its presence and know that your wise self has graced you with a symbol of ancient power and significance. Look deeply at what its meaning might be. Always remember a tree is only as strong as its roots, so dig deep while you reach for the sky.

What follows are some meanings of trees gathered over thousands of years from different cultures.

Alder: Strength

Almond: Promise

Ash: A sense of grandeur

Aspen: Goddess tree; overcoming challenges

Beech: Harbinger of prosperity

Birch: Gracefulness and new beginnings

Cedar: Purity and cleansing

Cherry: Beauty

Cypress: Transformation

Elder: Prosperity

Elm: Inner strength

Hawthorne: Glorious quest

Hazel: Inspiration

Holly: Fertility

Maple: Balance

Mimosa: Sensitivity

Oak: Strength and courage

Olive: Peace

Palm: Victory

Pine: Compassion

Redwood: Longevity

Rowan: Protection

Spruce: Hope

Vine: Connection

Willow: Sadness

This link to Native American tree symbolism has more:
www.warpath2peacepipes.com

Part Five

Tools

The expectations of life depend upon diligence;

the mechanic that would perfect his work

must first sharpen his tools.

~ Confucius

CHAPTER NINETEEN

Coaxing the Sandman: Tools & Techniques

A good tool improves the way you work,
a great tool improves the way you think.

~ Jeff Duntemann

If we don't take dreamwork seriously, or make the motions to commit, para-consciousness may not be able to successfully transmit symbolic messages. This is also true with other good intentions like diet and exercise—we have to take the necessary steps—this has been a recurring message in my dreams. Positive ongoing activity sends a signal to para-consciousness that you're serious, and then more information flows into your conscious awareness. What follows are time-tested and practical tools to help your process.

Dream Diary

The basic tools for working with dreams and synchronicities, depending what motivates you, are pen and paper, index cards, or your computer. I recommend creating and maintaining a *Dream Diary*, either in a journal, binder, spiral notebook, or your computer, so you can observe how guidance and patterns develop over time. As noted earlier, a simple but powerful tool for dream work is to keep a chronological *Dream Diary*, an ongoing journal of significant dreams and your work to interpret them. As also mentioned before, few dreams merit deep work, but when one is worthy of attention and analysis, recording the dream using the *Seven Steps in Dreamwork*© template is worthwhile. Referring back and reviewing symbols in hindsight reveal patterns.

People often overlook the importance of this step, believing they will remember key elements, or even the dreams themselves.

Keeping a *Dream Diary* sends a potent message to para-consciousness that you are paying attention to your dreams. Making your diary, and the practice of working with it enjoyable, reinforce that you're listening. The suggested *Dream Diary* template shown in Chapter 12 is a handy way to begin. It is remarkable what can be seen in hindsight, and this has been most amazing during the process of writing this book. Even dreams that stay with us lose detail over time, and when we go back and reread these dream stories later, new and deeper insights often emerge.

It's vital to record a dream as soon as possible to capture the symbols while the images are fresh in your mind. Some dreamers find it practical to keep paper, pen, and a small flashlight by the side of the bed. If you wake from a dream during the night, or early in the morning, you can capture key symbols—even a few words can trigger recall once you are awake and ready to record the complete dream. Others find it useful to speak into an audio recorder.

I am continually amazed by what I learn going back over dreams from months, or even years, earlier. Another benefit of recording dreams in chronological sequence is that patterns emerge. People, places, or objects show up repeatedly, creating themes and relating to Core Issues and recurring symbols that can lead to deep insight and healing.

Psychological studies in learning retention have proven the value of writing or typing the words whether it's studying for a test, memorizing lines for a play, or working with dreams. Something occurs in our brain circuitry as a result of getting the words down on paper, or in a computer, that relates to a dialog between the brain's hemispheres and memory. It's vital to record a dream while it is still fresh in your mind, capturing the main symbols and scenes as soon as possible. The story told earlier about Samuel Taylor Coleridge and his poem *Kubla Khan* powerfully illustrates this point.

The most basic and fundamental tools for dream work are pen and paper, index cards, or these days a laptop or tablet. Choosing a special vessel to be the container for your dreams packs an emotional punch. This may sound a bit mundane, but our minds can be subtle, and having something you look forward to using that feels easy and convenient is a potent symbol in itself. A designated place, not a random collection of Post-It notes, makes a difference. If my suggestion for a *Dream Diary* template appeals to you, by all means, make it your own. Use what works for you.

Decorating your *Dream Diary* with pictures, sketches, or images that illustrate your dreams, can evoke further meaning from dream symbols, and as described earlier, an image that depicts your dream's title is powerful. Engaging your creative side enhances your memory and likely improves recollection. Creating a container seems to enhance the quality of information you receive.

I find choosing a special book, blank journal, or loose-leaf binder to be a crucial part of the process. I choose a new one for each calendar year and select something that makes me feel good every time I pick up my *Dream Diary.* You can download the diary templates and an insert for a clear view binder at *www.SatiamaPublishing.com* or *www.JulieLoar.com.*

I also enjoy matching pens, and changing ink colors to suit my mood, as this engages both hemispheres of my brain and fires more circuits. Having said that, the important thing is recording the dream, just getting it down, not where or how. So, if you don't have a sexy journal handy, you can record your dream on any available material, including the proverbial cocktail napkin. In today's world we can even send ourselves a text or email.

Personal Symbol Dictionary

Symbols are quite literally the stuff that dreams are made of, and a good symbol dictionary is an important tool for dream work, the sleeping kind and the waking kind. If you are serious about working with your dreams, a good symbol dictionary points you toward meaning and can show common themes. Like the earlier chapters on symbols, a symbol dictionary is only meant to be a guide as You, the dreamer, are the ultimate authority where meaning is concerned.

Since dream language is symbolic, another valuable tool is to create a *Personal Symbol Dictionary* to keep track of symbols that repeat and are unique to you. You might repeatedly dream of your father, or a favorite high school teacher, and observing the context in which these symbols appear can be enlightening. Your symbol list can be part of your diary or kept in a separate record.

Because dreams are personal but contain universal, cultural, and individual symbols, augmenting a generic symbol dictionary with your own *Personal Symbol Dictionary* is a great way to deepen your dream insights. A *Personal Symbol Dictionary* is a step beyond as when you quite literally make symbols personal they contain more power. Like your diary, your personal dictionary can be accumulated in a spiral notebook or loose-leaf binder, an index card file, or as a computer file. Convenience, accessibility, and ease of adding entries in alphabetical order should be key features.

Whatever method draws you to keep adding to your personal dictionary is what will work for you. Adding personal interpretations and emotional responses is vital to a meaningful understanding. Your *Personal Symbol Dictionary* can also be used as a tool in free association and active imagery techniques. It's your dream, and learning to recognize and listen to the voice of your Soul is crucial—you decide what any symbol means.

Make your *Personal Symbol Dictionary* a resource you want to regularly add to. Some dreamers get really creative and decorate their personal dictionary with pictures, drawings, and images that illustrate the symbols. This really brings the symbols to life since we know a picture's worth a thousand words. This is why choosing an image to represent the dream is so powerful. The important thing is to create something you will feel motivated to interact with. Your own personal dictionary, like your *Dream Diary*, should be a treasure that beckons.

Later, you can add categories and subdivisions of areas that seem to emerge as special points of focus. As we look deeper into the characters in our dreams, we perceive what it is about them we are using to represent facets of ourselves. The more we play with this the more the Soul's symbolic language will speak to us with symbols we easily understand.

Your personal dictionary may include all three types of symbols: universal, cultural or collective, and personal. The notice and record when a certain symbol stands out in a dream, perhaps becoming the title and signature image as described in the *Seven Steps in Dreamwork*© process, noting recurring patterns and your emotional reactions. Watch for symbols that repeat and trigger a strong emotional response.

An example of ways your *Personal Symbol Dictionary* will expand involves how family members or friends become personal symbols. Over time we may notice that "sister Jane" always represents stubbornness, while "brother Joe" shows up in a dream to tell us we have been too aggressive. We may use the back yard of our childhood home to represent past happiness, sorrow, or lingering shadow material. Driving too fast in "our father's car" may mean we're dealing with authority issues. Our father might represent authority or responsibility, or the lack of it. Our mother could show nurturing, or not, and indicate a quality we need to express in waking life.

Usually, if we dream of the parent of the same gender, this represents the older wiser part of us. Here the voice of experience speaks. Likewise, if we dream of a child of the same gender, the message might be that we are acting immaturely in the area the dream addresses. Maybe the issue and its significance are still developing. We typically cast these actors in similar roles that repeat.

Deck of Dreams

Another creative technique to enhance understanding of how symbols speak to you personally, is to create your own *Deck of Dreams*. This can become a personal oracle deck. Collect images from photographs, greeting cards, magazines, or catalogs that appeal to you. Include any images you've chosen to represent titles of dreams you've worked with. This can also be a source for images in your *Dream Diary* and *Personal Symbol Dictionary*. Cut and paste them onto colored construction paper or poster paper and assemble your own deck. It's also possible to acquire blank playing cards to create your deck.

You can create your own oracle spreads when you have a question, or just to tune into symbols and images that have made a powerful impact from a dream. Gaze at the pictures and describe what emotions the images evoke. Make a note in your personal dictionary for future reference. By "bridging" the dream images into the waking dimension you strengthen your intuition. These cards can be used for personal and individual interpretation but any images drawn from magazines or online are often copyrighted and cannot be reproduced for other than your personal individual use. *www.SnappyGoat.com* has numerous free public domain images and many images on *www.Wikipedia.com* are public domain.

Draw the Dream

Some dreamers draw or sketch powerful pictures from their dreams as a way to process and understand the symbols. This was a significant part of the work of C.G. Jung who worked with mandalas as a process to interpret dreams. A Mandala, Sanskrit for "circle," is a graphical representation of the center. To Jung this meant the Self, or Soul. A mandala can appear in dreams and visions or be created spontaneously by drawing. Mandalas are present in many cultural and religious representations.

Other dreamers have made collages, or dream mosaics, drawing from their collected images. The creative process often brings more symbols to conscious awareness with the ability to feel the significance of emotional content. Sometimes the artwork evolves over time and key repeating symbols arise and change. Seeing the symbols in the waking state can connect the self-conscious mind more powerfully to the symbols and aid in interpretation.

Grounding a dream

Grounding a dream in waking reality is a practice thought to deepen understanding. The idea is to take some action, as described in the *Seven Steps in Dreamwork*© process, that imprints the symbols and brings the dream into the waking dimension. For example, if you dream of your brother, you might contact him the next day to say hello. Or if you have a dream about your grandmother, who died some years ago, you might journal about her and what she meant to you. You might look at some old family photos and allow your intuition to open. This sends a powerful message back to your Soul and para-consciousness that you're paying attention, taking heed, and applying your lessons.

In the next chapter I'll share a technique that can deepen your dream work by creating a virtual pilgrimage to an Oracle temple.

Julie Loar

CHAPTER TWENTY

Create a Dream Oracle Temple

Asking the proper question is the central action of transformation.
Questions are the key that causes the secret doors
of the psyche to swing open.

~ Clarissa Pinkola Estes, *Women Who Run With the Wolves:*
Myths and Stories of the Wild Woman Archetype

We learned at the beginning of the book that dream oracles and healing temples, such as those of Asklepius, existed at sacred sites in the ancient world where pilgrims traveled, seeking dream interpretation, healing, or guidance in major life decisions. In antiquity a pilgrimage was a major undertaking, often potentially dangerous, and requiring considerable investment of time and resource. People traveled to these sacred places of power, healing temples, and oracle centers, seeking guidance from an Oracle.

These seekers were motivated by some deeply felt need to undertake the long and sometimes arduous journey. These pilgrimages were undertaken at considerable sacrifice and usually only once in a lifetime.

Temple of Asklepius in Rome, Villa Borghese; Jean-Christophe Benoist (CC-3.0)

People traveled great distances, enduring hardships we can only imagine, and with considerable investment of resources. They often prepared for years and were dedicated to getting the most from their journey. It's likely they carried strong intentions as they journeyed, and a great deal may have been at stake in terms of how they implemented the answers they received.

We don't have the benefit of dream oracle temples in our modern world, although health spas can offer the physical aspect of this work. I have been drawn multiple times to Egypt and Greece where I have been powerfully affected by the energies of these ancient places, longing to bridge these ancient traditions with the modern world.

Although it is my dream to build an Oracle Temple, I have found that it is possible to recreate the experience in the midst of modern life when seeking counsel on a spiritual question or any serious matter in your life. We can recreate the sense of being present in a sacred temple through the power of intention, visualization, and ritual. Like pilgrims from thousands of years ago, we can undertake an inner journey and make a symbolic sacrifice of time or energy to enter the sacred shrine of our inner hearts, opening to higher guidance. This practice is powerful because of focused intent.

You might choose a picture of a sacred site, like the one shown at the beginning of this chapter, or one of a temple that moves you, to invoke a sense of connection to the divine. Take care formulating the question, identifying the real issue and not just a list of symptoms. In order to get good guidance, it's vital to get to the heart of the matter. If you are uncertain about your question, you can set the intention to receive general guidance about your life path. You can also ask whatever you need to know most right now or to understand the true nature of a mental pattern that repeatedly magnetizes conflict or pain in your life. Openness of mind and humility of heart are the most important attributes of this work. If you decide to create this Dream Oracle Temple process, resolve to heed whatever counsel your dream provides.

Preparation

Set aside an evening to create the sacred space for your virtual pilgrimage. If you can create a safe space with adequate room, you might consider doing this practice with a few close friends so you can share interpretations and feelings in the morning. Write down your concerns, your hopes and fears, about this issue. Cultivate the same intention and attitude as if you are undertaking a meaningful journey to an ancient sacred site and let go of your judging self. Take time to consecrate the space where you will do your ritual preparations and cleansing. Be willing to undergo your own symbolic catharsis, as happened in ancient dream temples, as a way to augment your sense of preparation and intention.

Some helpful hints from people who have had success with this process:

- Plan for a good night's rest to allow maximum sleep cycles
- Eat sparingly at your evening meal and consume no alcohol or other drugs
- Take a warm, soothing bath before retiring
- Scent the water with aromatic oil such as jasmine or lavender.
- Turn the lights low and light a pure white candle or two.
- Surround your tub with crystals, especially amethyst, which is believed to open the higher centers of the mind
- Listen to calming and inspiring music while you soak
- Sip some relaxing chamomile or rose tea
- Still and quiet the mind, emptying the thoughts and concerns of the day
- Put on special sleep wear, like rich cotton pajamas, which feel nurturing

Dream Incubation

Imagine that you have traveled to a sacred site of your choosing, such as the dream temple at Delphi or an Asklepion temple, and prepare your mind and heart—clear your mind and open your heart. After your bath spend a few minutes asking for a dream, creating a positive expectation in your mind. Consciously state your question or request and release the words to a higher source—your Soul— meta-consciousness. Dream incubation is the same technique used at ancient oracles and healing temples, where dreamers strove to dream with conscious intention or with a specific question in mind. Typically, this is related to the Soul's purpose, or mission in this lifetime, or to seek counsel about a spiritual path. Willingness to listen is still the most important hallmark of the seeker.

When visiting an ancient oracle, pilgrims knew the power of the right question. And as Plato also knew, formulating the right question is critical to receiving a meaningful response. In fact, it may be the most important thing we can do when faced with any problem or question.

It's not until we know how to precisely frame the question that we are ready to hear the answer. In a sense we have to build a container to receive the response. Setting a specific intention, or formulating a question before retiring for the night, can set the stage to receive an answer in a dream. Record the question in your *Dream Diary*, and invoke guidance in whatever manner feels right to you. The idea is to plant a "seed" and let it grow through the magic of symbols from para-consciousness (subconscious).

A few thought-provoking, or "big-dream" generating, questions to get you started:

How am I blocking my potential?

What am I denying?

Where is the pain? Anger? Sorrow? Resentment? Loss?

Where is the love? Where is the joy? Anticipation?

Where is the promise?

What is my work? My service? My bliss?

What is next in my life?

What needs to be healed?

What needs to be reclaimed?

If there is nothing bothering you at the conscious level, or a Core Issue that you are aware of, ask only to understand what you need to know most. Prepare an affirmation of intention to receive this guidance. Imagine your mind like a blank slate or screen on which your para-conscious will create a compelling story, or moving picture, during the night.

Meditate before sleep, and gently repeat your question before you turn out the lights. If you don't have a specific question, reflect on this ancient maxim:

***

Ask • Wait • Listen • Act

***

In the morning

In case this process does not yield a new dream, you can choose a dream in advance that you've remembered for years, one that made a huge impact. You can work with that dream in the morning, as I find there are always more riches to be mined from Big Dreams that have remained vivid over time. Prepare your *Dream Diary* and the *Seven Steps in Dreamwork*© template to record your dream in the morning.

If you have a dream but can't really recall everything, don't lose heart. Be grateful for the experience and know that your path is a journey. Maybe you aren't yet ready for the changes your dream message requires. Rest assured that the message was received, and when the time is right the symbols will emerge into your conscious awareness.

If the Dream Oracle experience has blessed you with a dream that you recall, perhaps a Big Dream, start right away to work with your dream. Take the time you've given yourself and work with the *Seven Steps in Dreamwork*© process to capture the dream and the symbols to include in your *Dream Diary*. As you Record, Reflect, and Resolve, go deep into the process with intention to receive the message(s).

Once you feel complete with the journaling process, give yourself a gift and do something that grounds the dream and fills you with hope and optimism. Whatever your experience has been, have a celebration. If you chose to have the experience with a circle of friends, honor their dreams and guidance, rejoice together, and gratefully acknowledge the priceless presence of fellow travelers on this journey.

Even though the ancient temples are in ruins, there is something powerful about invoking their memory and the work we once did there. Your Dream Oracle Temple can be revisited whenever you choose, especially if you are working on a major question or issue in your life. Guidance always awaits in the innermost shrine of your heart and highest self. Never doubt that your Soul is listening.

Afterword: Journey's End

It's good to have an end to journey toward,
but it's the journey that matters in the end.

~ Ursula K. LeGuin, *The Left Hand of Darkness*

The journey of this book began in earnest before I fully understood what the task would entail, but that is the way of a quest. If we knew when we set out what we would face after we cross the threshold we might lose courage. There are always dark times of doubt as well as powerful moments of guidance and miraculous inspiration. My journey through this book has been characterized by both, but I have experienced firsthand the potential for transformation the process contains. I am not the same person who set out on this journey a year ago. And in the way of cycles and synchronicity, as I typed the final words of this book, I look out my window at a snowstorm in April, bringing the journey full circle.

As I look back, I realize that this year has been a rare adventure with all the hallmarks of a heroic quest. At the beginning, I crossed a threshold from my "ordinary world" and stepped into a magical realm. I was given profound guidance at the outset as well as help, inspiration, and impulses for growth along the way. At significant stages I was given a dream that spoke to me in powerful symbols. Sometimes, I felt challenged by the message and at other times profoundly encouraged. The experience of the Seven Steps dream, and the process that flowed out of me in response, was life-changing.

And while I was creating *Seven Steps in Dreamwork*© Ted and I would look back and realize he was building seven stone steps at his property that were inhabited by a scarab type beetle. Such synchronicities dazzled me, especially at moments when I doubted myself.

As I am continually reminded through the experiences in my life, spiritual disciples need to have discipline—that's the source of the term. As discussed in Chapter Four, our physical maturation happens automatically but our spiritual growth requires our participation and effort. The spiritual path demands courage, determination, and effort. We have to be humble and willing to go into the transformational fire—a tall order indeed.

The journey has taken me from theory to practice in a powerful way. As I finished the first draft and looked back, I knew with a deep sense of wonder that what I had written was indeed a journey that connected inner space with my outer world. Indeed, I feel that the larger purpose of this book, and the profound journey the writing has taken, have made clear to me the power of dreams as guides on our spiritual path. Once we know that we walk this Path with the humble heart of a true pilgrim, the timeless teaching of our dreams become like beacons, milestones, markers along the way.

I thank you, the reader, for taking this journey of discovery with me. We live in a time when technology can disconnect us from others and what matters most. Throughout this pandemic year we have digitally connected and reconnected through Zoom, and that has offered its own miracles, seeing the faces of friends and loved ones at a distance. Weddings, funerals, and baby showers through technology have transformed our beliefs of what is possible.

As I write the final words of this book, which in the miraculous manner of guidance has felt like an assignment, I look back in wonder, realizing that my deepest reconnection has been with my own eternal self.

It's been an amazing ride, not always easy, but filled with blessings and the power of faith. I believe I now have a wider perspective and a better tool box to work with my own dreams to guide me. May your own journey be blessed with bright guiding dreams and brave companions of the road.

Acknowledgments

Every author knows that many others help in different ways in the creation of a book. I am deeply grateful to those who have encouraged and supported me through this year-long effort. Thanks to my publisher Karen Stuth of Satiama Publishing who believed in the book's message and has given her tremendous support to the effort. Enormous gratitude and a sense of awe goes to designer and fellow author Sue Lion. Her brilliant cover design conveys the very heart of the work, and the interior design of the print book frames the work in a powerful way.

My profound gratitude and appreciation goes to my husband Ted Denmark, who carefully, and with expert editing skill and keen insight, has read and re-read every word. He has given feedback and valuable insight throughout the process, encouraging me when I doubted. Thanks also to early readers of preliminary drafts who offered feedback and inspired me to keep going.

I humbly thank my Guide, my Soul, and para-consciousness, who have offered magical and miraculous dreams, synchronicities, and serendipities that have shone symbolic light and profound guidance along this journey. As I look back, I am amazed at the twists and turns the journey has taken as well as unexpected revelations, insights, and moments of transformation that have marked the passage.

References

Alcyone, J. Krishnamurti, *At the Feet of Master,* Theosophical Society, 1911, London, http://www.theosophy.ph/onlinebooks/AtTheFeetOfTheMaster_JKrishnamurti.pdf

Andrews, Ted, *Animal Speak: The Spiritual & Magical Powers of Creatures Great & Small*, Llewellyn Publishers, Woodbury, MN, 2002, https://www.amazon.com/Animal-Speak-Spiritual-Magical-Powers-Creatures/dp/0875420281

Bailey, Alice, 24 books published by Lucis Trust, 1919-1949, London, https://www.lucistrust.org/store/category/alice_bailey_books_p

Blavatsky, Helena, *The Secret Doctrine*, Tarcherperigree, 1888, 2016 reprint, New York, NY
___*The Voice of the Silence Voice of Silence* – up to Arhat (4th Initiation) available online from the Theosophical Society, 1889, https://www.theosociety.org/pasadena/voice/VoiceoftheSilence_eBook.pdf
___ *Isis Unveiled*, Blavatsky Archives, 1877, https://blavatskyarchives.com/theosophypdfs/blavatsky_isis_unveiled_volume_1.pdf

Campbell, Joseph, *Hero with a Thousand Faces*, Campbell, Pantheon Books, 1949, New York
___*Myths To Live By*, Penguin Books, (Penguin Random House) New York, 1972, 1993
___*The Inner Reaches of Outer Space*, New World Library, Novato, California, 2002
___*Myths to Live By*, Joseph Campbell Foundation, New York, 2011
___*The Portable Jung*, Penguin Classics, 1976, London

Collins, Mabel, *Light on the Path: An Essay on Karma*, 3rd edition 1970, Theosophical Society, https://www.theosophical.org/files/resources/books/LightonthePath/LOTP.pdf

Cooper, J.C., *An Illustrated Encyclopedia of Traditional Symbols*, Thames & Hudson, March 1987

Jung, Carl, MD, *Psychology and Alchemy,* Volume 12 in *The Collected Works of C.G. Jung,* Princeton University Press, Princeton, New Jersey, 2014
___*Synchronicity*, Princeton University Press, 1960
___*Psyche & Symbol*, Princeton University Press, 1991
___*Man and His Symbols*, Doubleday, New York, 1964, Carl Jung Institute in Zurich, Switzerland. There are locations in New York, Chicago, and San Francisco. https://en.wikipedia.org/wiki/C._G._Jung_Institute,_Zürich

Newton, Michael, PhD, *Journey of Souls: Case Studies of Lives Between Lives*, Llewellyn, 1994

___*Destiny of Souls: New Case Studies of Lives Between Lives*, Llewellyn, 2000, Newton Institute, https://www.newtoninstitute.org/books/

Von Franz, Marie-Louise, *Dreams: a Study of the Dreams of the dreams of Jung, Descartes, Socrates and other historical figures*, Penguin Random House

___*On Dreams and Death: A Jungian Interpretation*, University of Michigan Press, Dexter Michigan, 1998

___*The Way of the Dream*, Shambhala Publications, Boulder, Colorado, 1994

___*Alchemy: an Introduction*, Inner City Books, Toronto, Canada, 1980

Wangyal, Tenzin, *The Tibetan Yogas of Dreams & Sleep*, Snow Lion Publishers, 1998

Walker, Matthew, PhD, *Why We Sleep: Unlocking the Power of Sleep and Dreams*, Scribner (Simon & Schuster), New York, NY, 2017

Wesselman, Hank, PhD, *Bowl of Light*, Sounds True, Louisville, Colorado, 2011, http://www.sharedwisdom.com/course/bowl-light

Web Sites

https://www.JulieLoar.com

https://www.SatiamaPublishing.com

Edgar Cayce – link to his dream dictionary, https://www.edgarcayce.org/the-readings/dreams/dream-dictionary/

Nassim Haramein – Resonance Science Foundation, https://www.resonancescience.org/about

https://en.wikipedia.org/wiki/Plant_symbolism

https://www.proflowers.com/blog/plant-symbolism-guide

https://www.amazon.com/Celtic-Lunar-Zodiac-Interpret-Your/dp/156718510X

https://beadage.net/gemstones/